The SUFFOLK we live in

PAUL FINCHAM

BARBARA HOPKINSON BOOKS

© Barbara Hopkinson 1983
First published 1976
Reprinted 1983

Barbara Hopkinson Books
Kingston Road
Woodbridge
Suffolk
Tel: 039 43 2099

ISBN 0 9507963 2 8

Printed in England by Galliard (Printers) Limited, Great Yarmouth

CONTENTS

FOREWORD

In recent years, increasing interest has been shown in local, as distinct from national, history. A county's history, however, cannot be properly understood unless it is related to national events. There was no shortage of Suffolk books in 1976, when I was asked to write this one, but I felt that it gave me the chance to try to show why the county looks the way it does, and how it functions, while at the same time providing a short chronological survey of Suffolk history in the light of British history in general. In the years since the original publication, I have had frequent encouraging comments, and I am delighted that Barbara Hopkinson has agreed to reprint it. I hope it will continue to be useful for anyone studying local history, as well as informative and attractive for those general readers who love and care for Suffolk.

Many people have shown generous interest in this book. Mr G. F. Cordy of Felixstowe has taken great trouble with photographic work on my behalf. At the County Record Office, Mr Vic Gray suggested suitable material and arranged for items from the Records to be photographed, which the County Archivist kindly allowed me to use. The staff at Ipswich Museum were good enough to organise several special photographs for me, and Mr R. Markham read and corrected my geological chapter. The staff at the Ipswich Reference Library were consistently kind in arranging for illustrations to be made available.

I have been grateful for the skill and knowledge of Mr G. St J. Hollis, who not only provided several photographs but also suggested the outline for the Wildlife chapter. Mr and Mrs Harry Wilton, as on previous occasions, placed their collection of Suffolk material at my disposal. I wish to thank Mr Medwyn Roberts, who designed the jacket, Mr George Bates who provided the map on pages 6 and 7, and the following people, all of whom have helped me in different ways: Messrs Rupert Bruce-Mitford, Stanley Butcher, Henry Clark, Kenneth Cooper, Alan Driver, Henry Ferguson, Adam Gordon, Bryan Hall and Arthur B. Whittingham, Mrs Gerald Curran, Mrs Edwin Smith, and Miss Jackie Cottie.

Throughout the book, in accordance with current practice, English measurements are followed by their approximate metric equivalents.

I have benefited in my work from the constructive criticism of Norman Scarfe, himself the author of a number of valuable books on Suffolk history and topography. If my book proves useful or enjoyable, it will be largely thanks to him.

PAUL FINCHAM
Woodbridge, 1983

ILLUSTRATION ACKNOWLEDGEMENTS

Page

Front cover
Framlingham Castle
(*Henry Davy*) *G. F. Cordy*

Title-page
Buck's prospect of Ipswich, 1741
Suffolk Record Office

8 Septaria nodule
Ipswich Museum

9 Red crag, Butley
Institute of Geological Sciences

11 Kersey
G. F. Cordy

12 Minsmere
G. St J. Hollis

13 Newmarket
Cambridge Evening News

14 Woodbridge Tide-mill
East Anglian Daily Times

15 Pin-mill
G. F. Cordy

16 Southwold
Edwin Smith

17 Bawdsey
G. F. Cordy

18 Dunwich
H. E. Wilton

19 Bronze axe-head
Author's collection

20 The Ipswich gold torques
Ipswich Museum

21 Head of Claudius
Warburg Institute

22 Slave shackle
Romano-British lead cistern
Ipswich Museum

23 Remains of Walton Castle, 1786
G. F. Cordy

24 Sutton Hoo helmet
Trustees of the British Museum

26 Excavations at Sutton Hoo
Norman Scarfe

27 Hadleigh Church bench-end
Munro Cautley Collection

29 Victim of Danish attack, Ipswich
Ipswich Museum
Ipswich seal
Suffolk Record Office

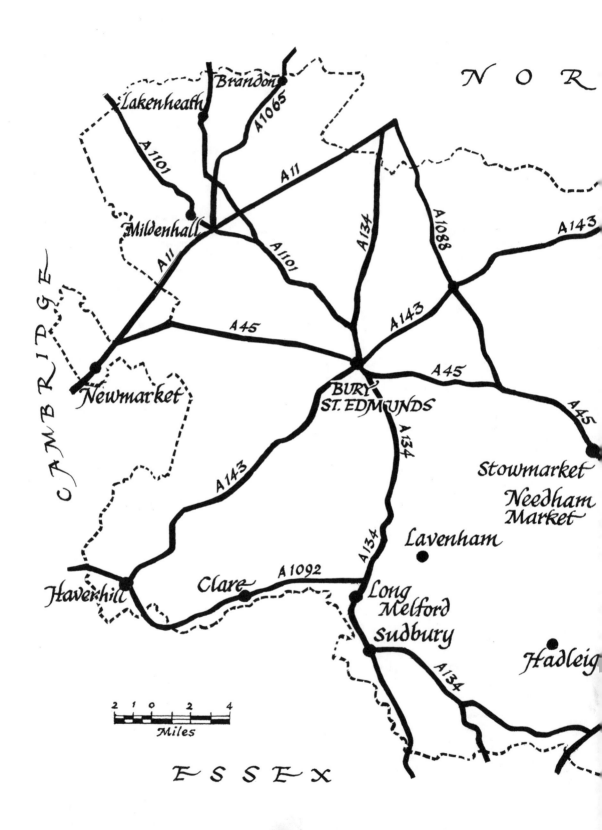

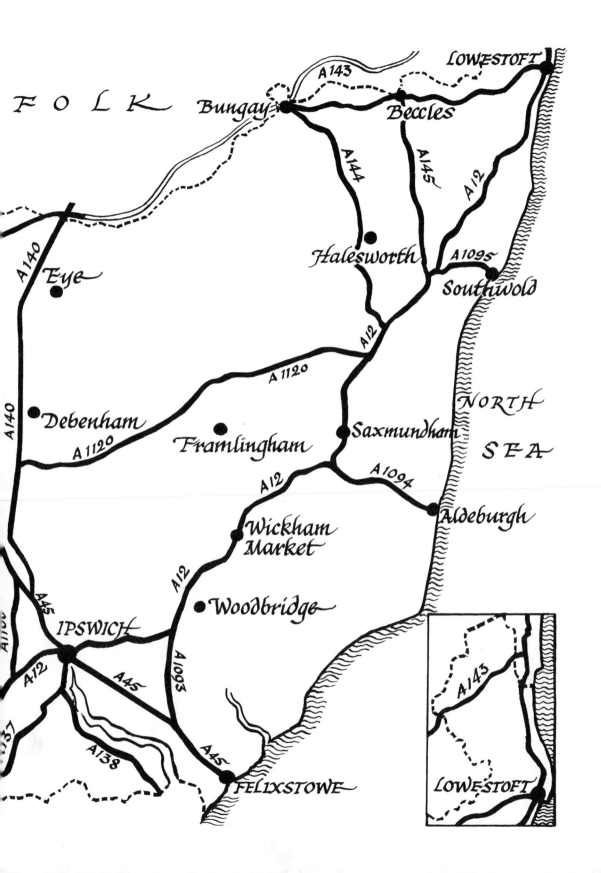

CHAPTER 1
THE GEOLOGY OF SUFFOLK

Suffolk's geological structure is comparatively simple.

Chalk forms the county's foundation – part of the great chalk belt which sweeps up from Berkshire and the Chiltern Hills to North Norfolk. The chalk was formed almost 100,000,000 years ago, in the Cretaceous period, when a chalky or limy sea covered much of what is now the British Isles.

After this there were many changes. The sea retreated, and the chalk was tilted, and worn away in parts, so that it was much thicker in some places than in others. In the Eocene period (50,000,000 years ago) the sea came in again. Over many thousands of years it deposited a belt of what we call 'London Clay' over the area from the River Stour to north of the River Deben. Fossils found in this clay, including sharks' teeth, suggest that the climate then must have been much warmer than it is now. The London Clay is a darker bluish grey, weathering to brown. A bed of curiously fractured limy mudstone within it, called 'Septaria', has been dredged up from the river estuaries and used as a building-stone. It takes its name from the way in which it is divided into many angular sections by cracks called in Latin *septa*. In the twelfth century a good deal of Septaria went into the building of Orford Castle, where it can still be recognized. In the nineteenth century, before the invention of Portland Cement, Septaria was often ground into a powder called 'Roman Cement'. There are some excellent examples of Septaria in the Ipswich Museum (see illustration below).

It was many millions of years before any further geological changes affected this area. The next series of deposits were laid down in the Pliocene and Lower Pleistocene periods, only a few million years ago. The names come from the Greek words: *pleion* = 'more' and *pleistos* = 'most' (referring to the age of the molluscs), and *kainos* = 'new', or 'recent'. These were the Crags. For some of this time, the southern part of the North Sea was dry land. The coast of southern England seems to have joined the coast of Holland and Belgium and so formed a large bay. Winds from the north and east blew across the sea, piling up sand and shells along the east side of the bay, which gradually silted up. The Crag sands were deposited in a series of layers. On the whole the older ones are in the south of the area and the newer ones in the north.

Study of the shell remains in the Crag indicates that these deposits were laid down in an age when it was becoming colder, as the Ice Age approached.

Coralline Crag is the oldest of the Crags. It is sand, full of the shelly remains of molluscs, particularly the Bryozoa which secrete a moss-like coral, sometimes called 'sea-moss'. Over the years, this Crag has hardened and cemented, forming a rock-bed which could be quarried for building-stone. The medieval towers of Chillesford and Wantisden churches have this Crag in them, and there is some in Eyke Church, and in Orford Castle again.

Apart from this small pocket, in the Boyton–Aldeburgh district, the rest of the Crag beds are more recent, laid down about 1,000,000 years ago. Red Crag, named from its bright colour, extends as far north as Aldeburgh. Beyond it, the Norwich Crag stretches up into Norfolk. Both kinds contain fossil shells, often in abundance, which give them that rough, craggy texture from which their name derives. In the Red Crag epoch the first elephants and horses appeared in this country. There were deer, leopards, and hyenas too, and members of the beaver family. Red Crag also contains coprolites, the fossilized droppings of mammals and fish. In the first part of last century it was found that ground-up coprolites made a valuable fertilizer (Chapter 16). Large numbers of fossils were obtained in the search for coprolites, and some famous fossil collections were built up at that time.

So much for the underlying, or 'solid', geology of Suffolk. But the shaping of the county was really done during the period of the Ice Age.

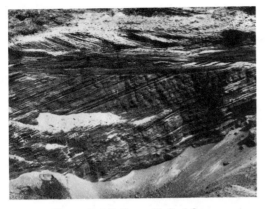

Crag-pit at Butley, with Red Crag

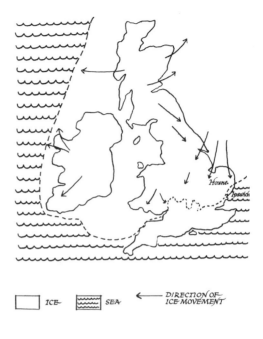

ICE [ ]   SEA ~~~~   ← *DIRECTION OF ICE MOVEMENT*

The Great Ice Age was not one single period of cold. The most up-to-date evidence suggests that, extending back in time, from about 10,000 years ago, there were a series of cold and warm spells, each lasting for about 30,000 years. In the warmer in-between spells, known as 'Interglacials', the climate was rather as it is now, or even milder. Men were living in what is now Suffolk in one of those Interglacial periods. The very first discovery that men existed in that early geological age was made in the 1790s in a brick-pit, now very famous, in Hoxne. One theory is that we are, at present, living in one of these Interglacials, and that conditions will steadily become colder and colder as we approach another phase of the Ice Age.

The snows of the north no longer melted in summer but were compressed into a great slab of ice. On several occasions – at least three and possibly four – the great ice-sheet slowly extended south. Its farthest extent seems to have been a line from the Bristol Channel to the Thames Estuary (see map on this page). This is known as the 'Lowestoft Advance'. When the ice-sheets moved, they dis-

placed and carried materials from the surfaces they travelled over: chalk and flints, clays and sands. Then, when the ice melted and retreated north again, much of this transported material, called a 'till', was left behind. Occasionally it was in the form of large boulders, or 'erratics'. When the railway line was being excavated between Ipswich and Bury St Edmunds, in 1846, several huge rocks – 2–3 tons (2–3 tonnes) each – were found in Norton Wood. They had to be removed with explosives. But for the most part, what the ice left behind in Suffolk was a spread-out layer of Boulder Clay, a rather heavy soil, with a lot of chalk and flint in it. This layer was weathered into a very rich soil-covering, varying in thickness from as little as 12 feet (3·7 metres) in the west of the county to well over 100 feet (30 metres) in the east.

The very last deposits of all have been the light sands and gravels of the eastern and western edges of Suffolk. These are still subject to climatic changes, being re-formed under our eyes in dust-blows, and by the unmanageable action of the North Sea.

Fossils from the Crag: mastodon tooth, whelk, coprolite, lobster's claw, shark's tooth

CHAPTER 2
THE LANDSCAPE REGIONS

THE LANDSCAPE REGIONS OF SUFFOLK

People whose acquaintance with Suffolk is slight sometimes speak of it as 'flat' but, as with Norfolk, this is far from true.

The county's landscape regions are closely related to the geology described in Chapter 1. The central two-thirds are covered by a layer of Boulder Clay. On either side of the clay belt, to the east and west, and in the Stour Valley to the south, there are lighter soils. It is an easy distribution to understand and remember (see map above).

THE BOULDER CLAY

This part is sometimes called 'High' Suffolk, a misleading name, for its height is mostly about 100–200 feet (30–60 metres) above sea-level. Even its highest point – at Depden, south-west of Bury – is only 420 feet (128 metres). So a better name for the Boulder Clay area is 'Central' Suffolk. The landscape is gently undulating, and you sometimes do get the impression of its being higher than it really is, when you follow a river-valley and climb on

to a plateau: for example, between the rivers Brett and Gipping at Bildeston or at Wattisham.

The whole county was originally a forest, before the time of human settlement, but, because of the rich clayey soil, this part was once covered with especially dense forest, and some of it is still wooded. Clearing the forest was a labour beyond the first settlers, with their primitive tools, and no real start was made until the Iron Age. Then a plough with an iron coulter was developed, so this fertile land could be properly cultivated. The Iron Age and Romano-British farmers began the task. Four or five centuries later, the Anglo-Saxons completed the clearance, creating pastures and cornfields out of woodland and scrub. When 'Domesday Book' was compiled in 1086, Suffolk was the most densely inhabited part of England, and most of the woodland had been conquered and cultivated. These central claylands had about seven times as many plough-teams at work as the lighter lands to the west.

10

In the Middle Ages, many of the fields were enclosed and drained by ditches leading into the valley streams. Good drainage is essential in this heavy clay area. Houses, too, were often built on a moated platform, to keep them sound and dry. In the twentieth century, tile drains are laid to make the clay fields as workable and productive as possible.

Wheat and barley are the principal cereal crops of the Boulder Clay lands. Since 1925, when it was introduced, sugar-beet has become very important and is grown in enormous quantities, to be sent to the sugar-factories at Ipswich and Bury. The fields on the whole are fairly small. But because modern agricultural machinery is large and expensive, and needs big fields to operate successfully and economically, farmers in several places (near Framlingham for example) have uprooted their hedgerows and filled in the ditches, to create great prairie-like stretches of farmland in this rich and fertile region.

THE SANDLINGS

The A12 highway marks the eastern edge of the clay belt. Between it and the sea is a wide strip of sandy gravelly lands. These are the 'Sandlands', or 'Sandlings', light and loamy, and drained naturally by many small streams. This was once famous sheep country, crossed by great sheep 'walks', but there are not many flocks now. Irrigation methods have been widely introduced since the Second World War, resulting in big improvements to crops, especially sugar-beet and potatoes.

Arthur Young, a Suffolk man who became Secretary to the Board of Agriculture during the Napoleonic Wars, praised the farming on the Sandlings. 'The most famous husbandry in this country', he wrote, 'is near Woodbridge, in the parishes of Eyke, Wantisden, Bromeswell, Sutton, Ramsholt, Alderton and Bawdsey.... Carrots are a crop that does them honour, on their rich, deep sand.' This is still true. Farmers in these villages still harvest great quantities of carrots.

Because of the lightness of the land here, a combination of a dry spell and a strong wind can produce alarming dust-blows. In March 1968 there were 4 foot (1·2 metre) drifts across the roads in Sutton, Butley, and Wantisden, and recently sown crops were blown out of the fields. Farmers are taking precautionary measures against a recurrence of this by planting lines of conifer trees as windbreaks. On some of the coastal heath between Woodbridge and Southwold, the Forestry Commission has planted three forest-blocks, mainly of Scots and Corsican pines, which grow quickly, and do well where the soil is poor and the rainfall low.

Some of the heathland has been reclaimed for cultivation. In the parish of Sutton, near the

Central Suffolk landscape, with Kersey Church

Coastal landscape – old drainage-pump at Minsmere

American air base of R.A.F. Woodbridge, land that in 1960 was covered with bracken and heather now produces healthy cereal crops. Most of the coastal marshland had already been reclaimed from the sea in the Middle Ages by building miles of earth banks called 'walls'. The great floods of 1953 led, later on, to thousands more acres of marsh being drained and turned into good grazing-land or arable fields.

THE STOUR VALLEY

This is a small area of valley gravels, exposed by the action of the River Stour, and settled very early by prehistoric people. The landscape here, too, is gently undulating, with little steep-sided valleys of the Stour's tributaries. Their waters governed the location of the cloth-fulling mills that were vital to the prosperous medieval cloth industry. Cattle now graze on the flood-plain of the Stour. The higher slopes above the streams produce good crops of

barley, potatoes, and sugar-beet. This beautiful countryside was made world-famous by the painter John Constable who was born at East Bergholt in 1776.

THE FIELDING, AND WEST SUFFOLK SANDS

An area of sands and chalky soils lies to the west of the clay belt. This is the region that was first reached by those prehistoric settlers who arrived from the Wash, or from the south via the Icknield Way, the old trackway that partly corresponds with the line of the A11 highway today. It was easier for them to clear the light woodland here and begin using the land for grazing. In the Fielding, from Bury to Newmarket, the lighter soil creates a chalky looking rolling landscape, its grassy slopes and ridges often crowned by strings of racehorses out exercising. The name 'Fielding' seems to have been acquired because this was an area that remained in open fields long after the rest of Suffolk had been enclosed. The western sands are sometimes called 'Breckland'. Those parts that are not now covered by great planted conifer forests provide an open, rather flat, landscape, broken from time to time by lines or clumps of tall pines, serving as windbreaks. Here, as in the coastal Sandlings, the wind sometimes whips up the soil and remoulds the landscape. A good example of this can be seen at Wangford Warren, near Brandon, where one of the reserves of the Suffolk Trust for Nature Conservation is a large area of sand-dune.

The diarist John Evelyn, in 1677, described 'the travelling sands that have so damaged the country, rolling from place to place...'. Another traveller, a century later, writing of the area round Brandon, wrote: 'We passed through an ocean of sand, scarce a tree to be seen in miles.' That is no longer true. Since 1922, the Forestry Commission has been hard at work here, planting great expanses of pine forest, sometimes edged with oaks or chestnuts to make them appear less formidable. The village of Santon Downham (almost overwhelmed by sand in 1668) is the Forestry Commission's Headquarters. In spite of all this, dust-blows are still a problem, and in 1968 some roads and ditches were blocked with sand so thoroughly that bulldozers and excavators had to be called in to carry out clearing operations.

Morning exercise on Newmarket Heath.

13

CHAPTER 3
THE RIVERS

The Boulder Clay belt running south-west to north-east across the middle of Suffolk is the main watershed of the county's two river-systems. From it, the River Lark and its tributary the Linnet, and the Blackbourn river, drain north-west into the Little Ouse, which runs west and north into the Wash. The other rivers – Waveney, Blyth, Minsmere, Alde, Deben, Orwell, and Stour – rise in the Boulder Clay, but all flow east, emptying themselves into the North Sea. All are fed by dozens of small streams, draining the heavy land of Central Suffolk.

Julian Tennyson, in *Suffolk Scene* (1939) says: 'Suffolk owes all the best part of her character to her rivers.' Their length and spread, 'make Suffolk a county of perpetual surprise'.

The Waveney, Suffolk's northern border with Norfolk, rises in Lopham Fen, close to the Little Ouse. Only a few yards of fen separate the two; on some maps they appear to be the same river. In its long, lazy journey to the sea, the Waveney

Woodbridge Tide-mill, newly restored

flows through beautiful countryside, perhaps at its best between Bungay and Beccles. In 1670 the river was made navigable as far as this: Daniel Defoe in *Tour Through the Eastern Counties* called it 'a considerable river and of a deep and full channel'. Fortunes were made in those two towns from water-borne trade. The navigation was closed in 1934. East from Beccles, the Waveney joins the Norfolk rivers, Bure and Yare, to meet the sea in one wide channel. The Romans must have made use of this system of waterways to build and supply their garrisons in the area.

Like most rivers, the Alde has no single source but has its origins in many ditches and drains over to the west of Framlingham. It approaches the sea, opening out at Snape, and so on to Aldeburgh. But its expected exit to the sea there is prevented by a shingle-bank and the long shingle-spit known as 'Orford Ness', about 11 miles (17·7 kilometres) long, which the 'tidal drift' action of the sea has built up gradually, since Roman times, by carrying down material from a little farther north. Because of the spit, and the shape of the mainland, the Alde turns sharply south, and flows parallel with the shore to reach the sea at Shingle Street. It is a favourite river with yachtsmen but, because of the shifting spit, access from the sea is variable. Sailing-boats occasionally find themselves stranded on the shingle-bank at the river-mouth after misjudging the point and time of entrance. In Suffolk, people usually get over the difficulty of distinguishing between the different tributaries (often approximately equal in length) of the various rivers by naming them according to the place from which they flowed. So the lower reaches of the Aldeburgh River, or 'Alde River', are sometimes referred to as the 'Orford River', or 'Ore River'.

The Deben, like the Alde, rises in a small way, a little west of Debenham, whose name it takes. Its importance, too, has always been linked with a shifting sand-bar at its mouth, just north of Felixstowe, and the size of ships which could cross it. The walls of the Deben Estuary were embanked from Norman times. By about 1600 this embanking had extended to Melton, and barges and schooners could reach Wilford Bridge. A scheme of 1818 to make the Deben navigable as far as Debenham, and so help farmers export their corn, came to nothing. Like the Ore and the Alde, the Deben now is very much a pleasure river, full of small craft, and with popular mooring-places at Ramsholt, Waldringfield, and Woodbridge.

Pin-mill on the Orwell – a favourite yachting centre

The Stour and the Orwell estuaries share a wide sea-mouth, flanked by the harbours of Felixstowe to the north and Harwich to the south. The Orwell is the most easily navigable of Suffolk rivers, ships can enter or leave at any state of the tide. The name 'Orwell' applies to the broad estuary from Ipswich to the sea. The river flowing into it rises from a spring called 'Orwell', in the village of Rattlesden, over towards Bury. But this river is not the Orwell, but the Gipping, for its whole length, from the village of Gipping right down to Ipswich. Ipswich stood at the corner of the estuary, and its old name, Gippeswick, seems to reflect that fact, since 'Gip' means 'corner of mouth'. It is not related to the river-name 'Gipping', as we have seen.

Arthur Young recommended that the Stour,

broad and shallow, with muddy bays, should be viewed when the tide was in. Others, especially the gulls and swans, like the muddiness. The Stour's upper reaches served the medieval clothing villages. After the river was 'improved' by Act of Parliament in 1705, it was a highway to the sea. Barges, each carrying 26 tons (26·4 tonnes), brought coal to Sudbury, through fifteen locks. The last barge used the river in 1930.

In the west of the county, the River Lark was made navigable as far as Bury St Edmunds in 1698. An ambitious plan to connect it with the Stour navigation, giving Bury access to the sea, came to nothing. Boats up to 88 feet (27 metres) long can still get as far inland as Mildenhall, and small ones even farther.

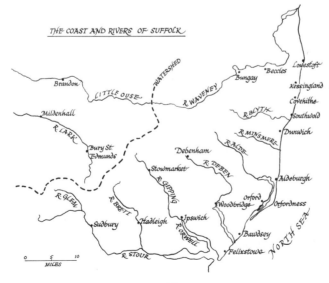

THE COAST AND RIVERS OF SUFFOLK

CHAPTER 4
THE COAST

Julian Tennyson observed that the real glory of Suffolk was the coast. Not for nothing has the whole Suffolk coast, from Kessingland in the north down to Felixstowe Ferry in the south, been designated one of the three Heritage Coasts of Great Britain (with Dorset and Pembroke). Because of the good fortune that estuaries and marshes precluded the growth of a coastal road, the visual and social injuries (caravans, bungalow shacks, etc.) sustained in the motoring age by so many beautiful stretches of the British shore from Cornwall to Yorkshire have been avoided. Now this designation means that the county's good luck can be consolidated by careful co-ordination between planners and conservationists and the general public.

Suffolk has about 50 miles (80·5 kilometres) of coastline, enormously varied: cliffs and estuaries, sand, shingle and mudflats, long empty stretches, with a character and a peculiar beauty of their own, owing their preservation to their relative inaccessibility.

This coast is continually changing, and being reshaped by the action of the sea. The high spring tides and north-westerly gales make inroads on the loose, sandy cliffs. Waves attack the cliff bases, undermining them and causing them to collapse on

to the beach, where the sea takes them away. The 'Chronicle' of Butley Priory records high tides and gales doing considerable damage early in the sixteenth century. In 1799 the poet Crabbe, of Aldeburgh, recorded eleven houses demolished at one time by a high tide.

The coastal marshland has always been subject to flooding. When this happens, certain higher lands, that were originally islands before the surrounding marshlands were drained and defended by earth 'walls' from the sea, resume their former character, as islands. The ending '-ey' on a village's name often indicates such an island site. Bawdsey, whose name means 'Baldur's island', is an example of this. We illustrate part of the earliest Ordnance Survey, where elevation of the land is shown by hill-shading. You can see how the village occupies higher ground, and would stand above the flood-waters if the sea came in.

Bawdsey, on the first Ordnance Survey map
(Opposite) Southwold

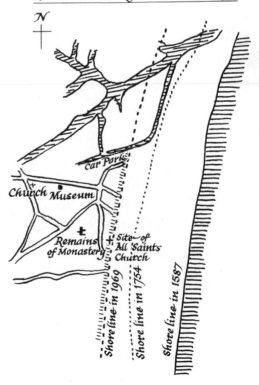

THE DISAPPEARANCE OF DUNWICH

17

Erosion is caused principally by 'tidal drift', the horizontal movement of the sea along the coast, with a scouring motion. The direction of this drift is to the south, and the eroded material has piled up in long shingle spits, or bars. We have already seen this, with the rivers Ore and Deben, in Chapter 3. It has happened at Felixstowe too. The part called 'Landguard' was once a long shingle-bar, where fishermen spread their nets to dry. In about the sixteenth century, it joined up with the mainland, forming Landguard Point, now built over.

How much land has actually gone into the sea is a much-disputed question, and there are exaggerated claims. But there is no doubt that, north of Southwold, Easton is now almost totally eroded. Its church went under water in the late seventeenth century. Covehithe near by suffered almost as badly. Its great church tower was preserved for a sea-mark; the nave and chancel were demolished in 1672. Dunwich was a prosperous seaport in the twelfth century, on a hill, some 40 feet (12·2 metres) above the sea. 'Domesday Book' recorded some early advances of the sea there. By 1350, 'upwards of 400 houses' had been overrun, as well as two of the nine churches. By 1677 the sea was flooding the market-place, and buildings were being pulled down to salvage their materials. The last of the medieval churches, All Saints, has gone into the sea in this century, after standing for many years on the cliff-edge, a picturesque and gradually disappearing ruin. The evidence suggests that the sea here has gained about a quarter of a mile (402 metres) in the last four centuries. Its advances continue still. The substantial hamlet of Slaughden, just south of Aldeburgh, has vanished in the twentieth century. The foundations of its last houses were still visible a few years ago.

Inundation of the coastal area continues. Since the last great floods of 1953, brought on by northerly gales, defence-works of various kinds have been carried out. Sea- and river-walls have been strengthened, shingle-banks have been pushed up by mechanical diggers. Much of this has been worth while, as further high tides demonstrated in the first week of 1976. But erosion seems to go in cycles, striking one part of the coast, then switching to another, so that long-term planning to combat it becomes difficult as well as expensive.

Dunwich – All Saints' Church in the early nineteenth century

CHAPTER 5
PREHISTORIC SUFFOLK

As we saw in Chapter 1, the first men were living in Suffolk in one of those Interglacial periods, about 300,000 years ago. This is what we call the 'Palaeolithic period', or – to give it its more common name – the 'Old Stone Age', when England was still joined to the Continent. Little is known about our Palaeolithic predecessors, though Suffolk has produced three of the most important sites in Britain: Hoxne, Mildenhall, and Ipswich (Foxhall Road). At the last site in 1855 a human jaw was found. It was taken to America where, unfortunately, it was lost, so cannot now be re-examined by up-to-date scientific methods.

These people must have lived the life of nomadic hunters, in temporary camping sites. There were elephants, rhinoceroses, bison, and various deer for them to hunt. They made crude tools and weapons from the flints which are so plentiful in East Anglia's layers of chalk. A lump, or nodule, of flint was struck with another stone, to get it roughly shaped. Then small shallow flakes were knocked from the surface, until an oval or pointed tool was obtained from the flint core. The small waste flakes were probably trimmed and used too. This way of breaking and shaping flints is called 'knapping' and it is one of our oldest industries. Brandon was, until quite recently, the flint-knapping centre of Britain.

The great majority of finds of this period came from the gravels in the river-valleys of the Waveney, Lark, Gipping, and Stour.

Next came the Mesolithic period, or Middle Stone Age. The woodland was spreading: there were birch and pine trees, and hazels and oaks on the heavy soils of Central Suffolk, but still little evidence of man's existence. Small mobile groups of hunters came from Denmark and Germany, for we did not become an island until about 5000 BC. They too made temporary camps with flint tools, while hunting the forest animals – deer and wild pig – helped by their hunting-dogs. They fished with barbed-bone spears, snared birds, and hunted the hare, fox, and badger for their fur. These men could not clear the woodland with such primitive tools. They lived rather in the treeless areas, such as the sand-dunes of the north-west, bordering on the fens.

By about 2500 BC, the first Neolithic, or New Stone Age, people were reaching these parts, some of them along the great prehistoric trackway, the Icknield Way, from Salisbury Plain to North Norfolk. They have been described as the first farmers on account of their rearing animals and growing crops. Their tools and weapons were still made of flint. For axes they shaped a flint blade and set it into a wooden handle. Scrapers, knives, choppers, and hammers were fashioned too. They were able to clear the woodland by burning it, but were without any means of turning over the extremely heavy Boulder Clay. Therefore, they preferred to live on the porous sandy soils, where the country was more open for grazing.

Theirs was still a nomadic way of life, with fishing, fowling, and a little cultivation, probably living in tents which they could easily move. At Lakenheath evidence has been found of a camp of some 328 × 115 feet (100 × 35 metres), which suggests that it was occupied by a number of families. There are the remains of hearths, fragments of pottery, and tools and bones.

One curious survival from the New Stone Age has not been excavated. This, at Stratford St Mary, is a 'henge' – a ditch inside an earthen rampart, with some kind of important central area. Like the more important stone henges, this may have been connected with some sort of ceremony of worship. Aerial photographs have also revealed a 'cursus', or ceremonial track, at Stratford, and another running beside the River Lark at Fornham.

Bronze axe-head from the Butley hoard

Knowledge of metal and how to use it came from the Middle East. The first metal objects were of copper, and blunted easily. Then it was found that an alloy, or mixture, of nine parts copper to one part tin, produced a stronger metal: bronze. It was scarce and expensive, and never ousted flint completely, for tools and weapons. The local chiefs naturally had first claim on the new metal. Itinerant smiths with portable furnaces used to travel over a wide area, melting down broken tools and re-casting them into new ones. The stock-in-trade of such a smith would be uncomfortably heavy for him to carry around so he sometimes buried a hoard of scrap-metal in an area where he knew he would be working, and where there was plenty of wood to fire his furnace. One such hoard, found in 1949 at Butley, between Woodbridge and the coast, consisted of more than seventy metal lumps and axe-heads, including the one illustrated on page 19. From these the smith would cast new axes, as well as bronze sickles for farmers, and saws and chisels for carpenters.

Some of our knowledge of Bronze Age people comes from their burial customs. They cremated their dead, placed the cremated remains in an urn, or beaker, of clay, perhaps roughly patterned with a thumb-print or piece of twig, and then heaped earth over the urn. The site of such burials is called a 'barrow', and about a hundred of them are known in Suffolk. A group of thirty-odd stands on heathland at Brightwell and Martlesham. Many more must have been destroyed by ploughing over the years, and now show up as circular marks in the fields where they stood, sometimes revealed only by aerial photography. One group of Bronze Age people in Suffolk practised urn burial, where the urns were not subsequently covered over with earth. Eight such cemeteries, or urnfields, were discovered in the Rushmere district of Ipswich.

The last group of prehistoric settlers are the men of the Iron Age. From about 500 BC, the pressure of an increasing population encouraged some of them to leave their homes in North Germany. They brought improved methods of agriculture and a knowledge of using iron, harder and more effective than bronze. In the third century BC, more warrior-like men came over from France. One, whose skeleton was found at Mildenhall, was buried between two ponies, with his long iron sword, axe,

and a gold necklace. Later still, about 100 BC, came the Belgic tribes, squeezed from France by their Roman conquerors – soon to come here too. They introduced the potter's wheel, and better ploughs with iron coulters, capable at last of creating farms on the rich, heavy soils. One group settled to the west of the clay-belt woodland and became the Iceni. Others, in the Stour Valley, were the Trinovantes with a great earthwork fortress at Clare.

These Iron Age people were the most sophisticated of the prehistoric age. Impressive collections of rich, elaborately decorated objects of this period have been found, both by chance and in archaeological excavations. Their introduction of coinage, to replace the old way of barter, is substantiated by the discovery of gold and silver coin-hoards. Westhall has yielded a collection of bronzed and enamelled harness, clearly the property of a chieftain. 'Developers' and their bulldozers are often, and rightly, criticized and blamed for the wholesale destruction of potentially valuable archaeological sites, but it was in fact an operation of this nature which unearthed Suffolk's richest treasure of the first century BC. In October 1968, while he was working on the Belstead Hills Estate (illustrated below) at Ipswich, the driver of a mechanical digger brought up five splendid gold torques, or necklets, each weighing 2 lb (0·9 kg). Another was found, two years later, in a garden near by. All had obviously come from the same workshop, and they were not all finished: on some, the looped terminals lacked their final decoration. Only a king or high priest would have aspired to such objects. The Roman historian Dio Cassius described one worn by Boudicca, Queen of the Iceni. The Ipswich torques were probably concealed in an emergency by a goldsmith, who did not live to recover them.

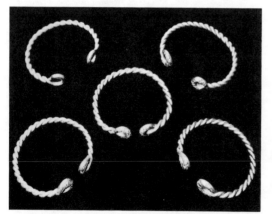

The Ipswich gold torques and the site where they were found

CHAPTER 6
ROMAN SUFFOLK

When the Romans began their conquest of Britain in AD 43, the great Belgic chieftain Cunobelin had established himself at Colchester. His capital, on the slopes to the west and south-west of the present town centre, was in effect the capital of Britain. The Romans regarded its capture as their decisive victory and established their first legionary fortress on the hill-top site above. This was their capital for a short time, and the focus of their earliest road-system. To the natives of Suffolk it seemed uncomfortably close.

Suffolk was inhabited principally by two groups of native people. Over in the north-west, in a fairly compact area to the west of the clay belt, and going on into Norfolk, lived the Iceni (whose name was pronounced Ickeni). The present-day place-names of Icklingham, Ickworth, and Ixworth must be associated with that tribe and so must the old trackway, the Icknield Way. The eastern side of the clay belt, in the Stour Valley, and extending down through Colchester, was the home of the Trinovantes, the tribe defeated by Cunobelin and then subjugated by the Romans.

After the Roman occupation, Prasutagus, the Iceni leader, welcomed the conquerors as allies in his struggle with his western neighbours, the Catuvellauni. He accepted the status of a client king, which allowed him to retain his title and position, but gave the real administration to a Roman official, the Procurator, Catus Decianus. Hoping to ensure a peaceful succession after his death, he bequeathed half his property to the Roman Emperor, the rest to his wife Boudicca, and his two daughters.

The Trinovantes had gained nothing from the conquest. Some of their best lands were taken from them, to provide a *colonia* at Colchester: the Roman way of rewarding retired soldiers was to give each one a parcel of land. The Trinovantes were, in addition, made to help with the building of a colossal temple at Colchester, for the worship of the Emperor Claudius, and taxed to help pay for its upkeep, its priests and ceremonies.

When Prasutagus died in AD 60, the Procurator behaved greedily and foolishly, seizing the dead King's property, allowing his family to be insulted and ill-treated, and arresting some of the leading Iceni families. His behaviour roused Boudicca to savage rebellion. At the head of a great mob, its ranks swollen by the resentful Trinovantes, she marched on Colchester, slaughtered the Romans, and destroyed all signs of their occupation there, including the temple. Her victorious army went on to London and St Albans where it caused similar havoc before being caught and crushed by the Roman legions at a battle somewhere in the Midlands.

The Romans took a terrible revenge. Large numbers of Iceni tribesmen were deported in labour gangs, to work on fen drainage. Many were put to death and their lands laid waste. It was some years before, under a more enlightened governor, they could begin to rebuild their lives and their economy.

In the River Alde, in 1907, a boy, fishing, found the head of a statue of the Emperor Claudius. It seems likely that it came from the statue known to have stood outside the Colchester temple: someone may have taken the head as loot. When the revolt collapsed, the thief, not wishing to be caught with such incriminating evidence, threw it into the stream, where it lay undiscovered through nearly 2,000 years. It is now in the British Museum.

Bronze head of the Emperor Claudius

Slave shackle

The Roman organization of Suffolk seems to have been planned, after Boudicca's defeat and suicide, to ensure that nothing like it could happen again. Suffolk was very much a thoroughfare. Just over its southern border was, after its rebuilding, the *colonia* of Colchester. To the north were two towns, Caistor-by-Norwich and Caister-by-Yarmouth, and to the west, Cambridge and Chesterford. Suffolk lay between them all, crossed by a network of connecting roads, along which troops could be moved if and when required. Evidence suggests at least 400 miles (644 kilometres) of Roman roads in the county. They were less substantially built than roads in some other regions, where there was local stone available, and usually had no more foundation than a gravel bed of 17·7 inches (45 centimetres). They were seldom completely straight, although long straight stretches of them have been incorporated in our modern road-system, between Halesworth and Ilketshall for example, shown on the Ordnance Survey Map as Stone Street. Over in the west, the Bury–Kentford road follows the Roman line. So does much of the A140 between Ipswich and Norwich. Study of the Ordnance Survey Maps will reveal a surprising number of lengths of Roman roads, and provide a framework for the settlement pattern.

There were no towns, but small settlements grew up at strategic points, in river-valleys, and where one road crossed another. They were local markets, or staging-posts, or centres of a local industry. At Wattisfield, where the Boulder Clay woodland provided ample fuel for firing, more than twenty pottery kilns have been found of the Roman period. It is interesting that Wattisfield is still the centre of a local pottery manufacture today. The most important crossing-point was Combretonium (Coddenham), which grew where the London–Colchester–Caistor road crossed the route from Cambridge to the east, leading through Hacheston, another Roman industrial site. The remains have been found, in the Coddenham neighbourhood, of a small number of villas, or country farm estates: Eye, Stonham, Whitton (near Ipswich), and Capel

St Mary. None of these has been thoroughly excavated, to provide a clearer picture of rural life under the Roman occupation. Not long ago, aerial photography revealed the site of a large, imposing villa, with its detached barn, at Lidgate, near Bury. Its excavation at some future time might add considerably to our knowledge. It may have been a similar villa whose owners were buried in four great mounds near the junction of Rougham, Rushbrooke, and Bradfield, in West Suffolk, along with some of their possessions. The iron shackle, with chain and padlock (see illustration on this page) recently unearthed at Debenham is a grim reminder that slavery existed in the Roman Empire, and that country estates like these probably relied upon slave-labour for much of the field-work.

We need to remind ourselves that Roman rule in Britain extended over four centuries – as long as from the Age of Elizabeth I to our own times. It has, therefore, left behind traces of four centuries of developing civilization.

It was the third century AD before Roman Britain, and Roman Suffolk, was subjected to threats from outside, as Anglo-Saxon raiders from the Continent began to menace and plunder our shores. Ten great fortresses were built, from the Wash to the Solent, to guard that vulnerable stretch of coast, known as the 'Saxon Shore'. The mouth of the Waveney and its associated Norfolk rivers was overlooked by Burgh Castle (Gariannonum), with huge walls, solid corner-bastions like drums, and spring-guns mounted upon them. In Suffolk, Walton Castle, between the Deben and Orwell estuaries, presided over the seas. It has gone into the sea itself now, but as recently as two centuries ago there was still almost 650 feet (200 metres) of wall left, 9·8 feet (3 metres) thick, and innumerable Roman objects have been found in the vicinity. Sometimes, at very low tide, the last fragments of its walls and towers are seen a little way out to sea.

Lead cistern from Icklingham – note the Christian (chi-rho) symbol

Thus guarded, Suffolk remained relatively secure when other areas were troubled. The year 367 was critical for Roman Britain. She was invaded on all fronts by barbarian attackers, and a leader – Theodosius – had to come from Rome to restore order and morale. Even so, the villa at Whitton was occupied as late as 395. The insecurity of these times is revealed by a number of treasure-hoards: people in danger buried their valuables, hoping to retrieve them when the crisis had passed. Pots of coins are fairly common, but Suffolk's greatest treasure of this time is the collection of thirty-four pieces of handsome silverware, found at Mildenhall in 1942 by two men ploughing. One dish alone weighs more than 18 lb (8·2 kg). The silver must have been the prized possession of a rich Romano-British family. There are Roman remains near by, possibly their villa home. It seems likely that they slipped out, when raiders were in the neighbourhood, to conceal their wealth. They never recovered what they had buried, and it is not hard to imagine why.

Some of the spoons in the Mildenhall Treasure bear the Christian symbol. So does the lead cistern (see illustration on page 22) of the fourth century, found with two more at Icklingham. It may have been used as a baptismal font, indicating that Christianity was practised in at least one part of Suffolk after the Emperor Constantine permitted it in 313. But when times were troubled, towards the end of the fourth century, many people must have turned back to the old religion, worshipping the gods of their forefathers.

The remains of Walton Castle as they appeared in 1786

CHAPTER 7
ANGLO-SAXON SUFFOLK

The Roman occupation of Britain did not end suddenly. Throughout the fourth century, more and more troops were withdrawn to help defend their Empire's frontiers. Others defected to support rival claimants to the imperial throne. Britain's consequent weakness coincided with the period of most severe pressure from outside. By about 410, the province was on its own. A plea for help to the Emperor Honorius produced the reply that they must organize their own defences.

The next hundred or so years is perhaps the darkest part of that time we call the 'Dark Ages'. Archaeologists are shedding more light on them, but the darkness is still formidable. In some places, as the Roman order gradually broke down, groups of mercenary soldiers, called *foederati*, were invited in from northern Europe, to help with the business of defence. The inevitable happened. They tended to take over the leadership in those towns and settlements they were defending, and sometimes asked fellow tribesmen from their homelands to come and share the territory with them. So the collapse of Romano-British culture and control, and the earliest settlements by Anglo-Saxons, are closely related.

It seems likely that, in Suffolk, in the populous Ixworth and Coddenham areas, mercenaries like these were in command in the fourth century. Meanwhile, migrant farmer-settlers were arriving along the shores, perhaps via the Wash, or along the Icknield Way. In the 1960s and 1970s, on the heathland at West Stow, in the valley of the River Lark, a large pre-Christian Anglo-Saxon village has been excavated, and some of its huts reconstructed on their original sites. The remains owe their preservation to the fact that they have never been built over by later settlement, which would have destroyed the evidence, as it has done in so many places. There are sixty hut sites, in three groups, with a larger hut to each group. The builders plainly had some skill in carpentry: the huts had plank floors, the space below being used as rubbish-pits, in which the discarded bones of pigs, sheep, and oxen have all been found by archaeologists. Two huts had been used for weaving – the loom-weights were found, as were enormous numbers of bone combs, some double-sided for wool-combing. Pottery was made on the spot, so this village must have been largely self-supporting. A quantity of coins of the late fourth century suggest that it was continually occupied from the Roman period onwards, and that

it was abandoned in the seventh century, when a Christian church was built half a mile (0·8 kilometre) away, and became the nucleus of a new settlement.

In the east of Suffolk, about the year 500, a more war-like family came from the Uppland district of Sweden, crossing the sea in their long clinker-built boats. They sailed up the Deben to settle in the Ufford–Rendlesham area. Their leader was called Wuffa, and the Wuffingas (the word means 'offspring of Wuffa') provided the ruling family of the kingdom of the East Angles. Ufford means 'Wuffa's ford', or river-crossing.

By 600, Wuffa's grandson, Raedwald, had 'won pre-eminence for his own people', as Bede puts it in his *History of the English Church and People*, and he himself won the title of 'Bretwalda', and became overlord of all the provinces south of the Humber. He was baptized into Christianity during a visit to the Christian King of Kent, about 620, but he none the less took the precaution of setting up in his hall, or palace, two altars – one to the Christian God, the other to the old gods.

Raedwald's successors placed Christianity on a sounder footing. In the early seventh century, missionaries came to organize the conversion of East Anglia. St Felix established himself at Domnoc (probably Dunwich), and Fursey, an Irish missionary, occupied the old Roman fort of Gariannonum. St Botolph founded a monastery at Icanhoe (possibly Iken) on the River Alde. But the kings who followed Raedwald on the throne lacked his qualities of leadership. Four of them perished in battle in quick succession, and after them East Anglia was never again more than one of the minor kingdoms.

It was Raedwald – who died, more pagan than Christian, in 624 or 625 – who was buried in that astonishing Anglo-Saxon royal cemetery at Sutton Hoo. The group of mounds, a dozen or more, stood above the Deben, not far from Rendlesham where we know there was a royal palace, though its exact site remains in doubt. One of the mounds, 12 feet (3·7 metres) high and 100 feet (30·5 metres) long, was opened in the summer of 1939. It had covered a ship, 86 feet (26·2 metres) long and with places for thirty-eight oarsmen, which must have been hauled up from the river and lowered into a cavity before being covered over. In a cabin amidships were priceless treasures, put there for Raedwald's use on his journey to another world. Forty-one gold and

(Opposite) The Sutton Hoo helmet after its final restoration

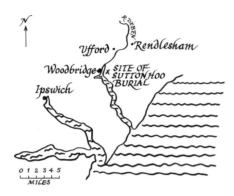

SITE OF THE SUTTON HOO SHIP-BURIAL

jewelled objects testified to his importance. A helmet, shield, sword, javelins and spears, showed him to have been a warrior. The cauldron, the vast drinking-horn, the bowls and spoons, were meant for lavish junketings in the next world.

More than a thousand years in the sandy soils of East Suffolk had corroded some of the objects. The ship, too, was decomposed, and only its ghost-like shape, and rusty nail marks, were left. There was for a long time some doubt about whether or not a body had ever been in the ship, and – if so – where

it was. Now the experts have decided, from the evidence of coins, and scientific tests, that this must be the grave of Raedwald. Only a truly pagan ruler, respected and feared as Bretwalda, would have had so rich a funeral-ship as the one buried at Sutton Hoo: the richest royal burial of this period known in Europe.

For two centuries after Raedwald the East Anglian kingdom was less dominant, and got on with more fundamental things. Christianity triumphed: Dunwich was the bishopric for the whole of East Anglia until the 680s, when Norfolk got its own see. By the end of the eighth century, villages, churches, and parishes, were all established, according to the evidence of place-names. There were even the first beginnings of town life. The Anglo-Saxon Chronicle mentions Suthbyrig (Sudbury) in 798. Ipswich was a trading-centre, and pottery called 'Ipswich Ware' was made there.

This was the picture when, in 841, trouble came: the first recorded raid by the Danes and the start of another unsettled period. The Danes were tough, ruthless men – a well-disciplined fighting force. By 865, sporadic raids had given way to a large-scale landing in East Anglia, the smallest and weakest of the kingdoms of England. The Chronicle called this a 'great heathen army'. It was commanded by Ivar the Boneless.

Archaeologists at work on the Sutton Hoo ship in 1966

26

After their first successes the Danes went north for a few years, then returned in 869. On 20 November that year they captured and murdered Edmund, King of East Anglia. Many legends have grown round Edmund's story. His martyrdom took place at Haegelisdun, probably just outside Norwich, but Hoxne in Suffolk later claimed to have been the place, and still boasts a monument to support its claim. In the accepted folklore, the King was tied to a tree and shot with arrows. His head was cut off and thrown into a wood, where his followers subsequently found it between the paws of a wolf (see illustration below). They 'applied all their skill and ability to fitting the head on to the body . . . and committed them, joined in this way, to a suitable tomb. Over it, they built a primitive chapel, where the body rested for many years.' There is more about the Edmund legends in Chapter 10.

This was East Anglia's answer to those rival tales of heroism stemming from Alfred's exploits in Wessex. Edmund became venerated as a saint and a resistance leader against all forms of tyranny.

The Danes came again to East Anglia in 879 and, under their leader, Guthrum, they 'occupied that land and shared it out'. There are very few place-names, however, that have Danish origins, for the good reason that this part was already largely settled before their onslaughts. They were content to control. Risby, near Bury, is a Danish name, and presumably denotes a Danish settlement. So is Eyke, which means 'a settlement in the oak woods'. Ellough, in north-east Suffolk, means 'heathen temple'. Apart from these, there are some interesting Anglo-Danish mixtures, probably indicating that Danes and English lived together in the same settlements: nothing very extensive. Kettlebaston and Bildeston, for instance, are made from a Danish personal name placed before the Anglo-Saxon '-ton' or '-tun', meaning 'a settlement'. The Danelaw, that part of England under Danish rule, extended from the Thames to the Mersey, and although Alfred of Wessex and, later, his son Edward, reconquered it by 920, Danish laws and customs remained. The rest of the tenth century was a time of consolidation and prosperity, with English and Danes sharing the same interests. When further fleets of Norsemen attacked, these East Anglian Danes regarded the new invaders as the intruders.

Ipswich was attacked from the sea in 991, by 5,000 men on their way south, where they fought the Battle of Maldon, in Essex. In 1010 more Danes, under Thorkell the Tall, landed at Ipswich before going on to fight at Ringmere in Breckland. The skeleton (see illustration on page 29) of a man found at Cox Lane, Ipswich, in 1961, probably belongs to one of these attacks. Sword-cuts are visible on his skull and leg, and the skull is scorched

from burning timbers in the pit into which his body was flung. These savageries ended when a Dane, Sweyn Forkbeard, and his son Cnut (Canute) after him, became kings of England.

In spite of centuries of warfare and destruction, there must – between spells of fighting – have been steady social and economic progress. For when William of Normandy came to the throne in 1066, he ordered a survey of his new realm to be made. This, the 'Domesday Book', shows that Suffolk, in 1086, was the most densely populated part of England. There were 417 churches (four out of every five of Suffolk's medieval parish churches today) and 178 water-mills, which gives an idea of the extent of arable farming. More than 2,400 estates, or holdings of land, are listed: most of the woodland, brought under cultivation at last, had given way to arable fields and pastures. The county's average population seems to have been about ten to twelve people to the square mile. Population distribution was, of course, uneven. The district to the north of Ipswich had seven times as many people, and seven times the number of plough-teams at work, as the sandy area in the north-west, over towards Breckland. Perhaps most revealing of all is the information that Suffolk had 7,460 freemen (who owed feudal services to no one), more than half the total for the rest of England. At least nine Suffolk towns had markets – several more than any other county.

Towns were still small: about 3,000 people at Dunwich, the same number at Bury; 1,300 at Ipswich, which had suffered a nasty setback. But the towns were growing rapidly. At Bury, between the Norman Conquest and 1086 when 'Domesday Book' was compiled, 342 houses were built.

A bench-end in Hadleigh Church.

CHAPTER 8
EARLY IPSWICH

The Romans had a villa at Castle Hill, at Whitton. There was an Anglo-Saxon settlement on the west bank of the Gipping, with a large burial-ground between the Hadleigh and London roads. But the beginnings of Ipswich on its present site can fairly confidently be dated to the seventh century.

A certain kind of pottery – Ipswich Ware – provides some clues. The kilns which produced this on an industrial scale have been excavated in Cox Lane, at the back of the Co-operative Society's shops. This pottery has been found in many places all over eastern England, suggesting that, even as early as this, Ipswich was a trading-settlement, and probably in contact with the Continent.

A bottle found in the Sutton Hoo ship-burial has been identified as Ipswich Ware. At the point where the Town Hall now stands, on the Cornhill, there was in the Middle Ages the Church of St Mildred. That name indicates a very early foundation, for Mildred died in about the year 700. It is possible that the Wuffingas, the East Anglian ruling house, had a palace, or hall, here too, making the town one of the royal administrative centres of the East Anglian kingdom.

So there was an industrial site to the east, and a royal hall to the west, of the present town centre. Between them, where the main streets of modern Ipswich run (Carr Street and Tavern Street) grew the first settlement in the town. Its Anglo-Saxon name was 'Gipeswic'. This means 'the collection of dwellings' (wic) 'at the corner, or bend, of the mouth' (gip) of the River Orwell.

These were unsettled times. In 885, the mouth of the Orwell and Stour rivers saw King Alfred's ships in action against the Danish fleet. In 991, and again in 1010, Vikings 'harried' Ipswich on their way to battles elsewhere. Such events encouraged the people to organize some sort of defences for their town, by digging a ditch 20 feet (6·1 metres) wide and 5 feet (1·5 metres) deep, curving round the part of the town which had been built up, more or less along the line followed by Crown Street and St Margaret's Street now. It was only a ditch. Not until the troubled times of King John, in 1203, was an earth rampart built up over it, giving the name 'Tower Ramparts', which still survives, to that part. The ditch, and later the rampart, enclosed the town through the period of the Middle Ages, and gave it its distinctive shape, still retained by the central area.

By 1066, Ipswich was a prosperous settlement. Its boundaries extended from Westerfield and Whitton in the north to Nacton, Wherstead, and Belstead in the south. Stoke Bridge and Handford Bridge already bore those names by 970. The town had 538 burgesses. Some got their living from trade, others were farmers, cultivating land as they cleared it, and grazing animals. They paid rent – in both cash and honey – to Queen Edith, wife of Edward the Confessor, and her brother, Earl Gyrth. At this time there were certainly ten churches, probably eleven. Holy Trinity stood where Christchurch Mansion now stands. St Augustine's was in Stoke, across the river, and St Michael's between the town centre and the river. St Lawrence's, St Stephen's, and St Peter's were as they are now. The two churches of St Mary were, presumably, St Mary Tower and St Mary Elms. Just over the borough boundary, in Thurleston, was the Church of St Botolph. The tenth was St Julian's. We know that St Mary's at Stoke existed in the tenth century, so it, too, can probably be added to this list.

Twenty years later, when the Domesday Survey was made, Ipswich presented a very different picture. Three-fifths lay waste, another fifth was much depressed. Only 110 burgesses were in a position to pay their customary dues, and 100 more paid only one penny each, and 328 homes which had previously paid taxes to the King were no more. It seems that Ipswich, like Norwich, was associated with the East Anglian Earl, Ralph Guader, in his unsuccessful plot against William the Conqueror, in 1075. As well as the town's dilapidation, the earldom of East Anglia was suppressed for a time after this, and the town's administration passed into the hands of Roger Bigod, the Sheriff, who governed it 'in the King's hand'. Roger's son, Hugh, was re-created Earl in 1140, by King Stephen who then had to besiege him in about 1153, at the Castle of Ipswich. It seems to have been one of a group of 'adulterine' castles put up by unruly and greedy barons during the troubled period, known as 'the Anarchy', when Stephen and Matilda were fighting over possession of the throne, and superseded by Orford and Bungay. The site of Ipswich Castle has not yet been determined, either by documentary or archaeological evidence. One likely site is in the Arboretum, opposite the Ipswich School in Henley Road. Wherever it stood, the Castle was razed to the ground in 1176 by Henry II, when he was bringing the rebellious barons of his realm to order.

The town had so many natural advantages that it

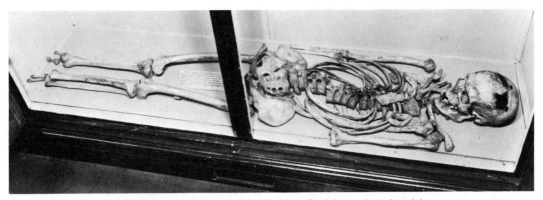

Skeleton of a man probably killed in a Danish attack on Ipswich

soon recovered from these setbacks. There was a good harbour, and plenty of fresh water. The names of Brook Street, Spring Road, and St Helen's Wash (now St Helen's) show where that water-supply came from. There was expansion after the troubles of 1075. Two priories of Austin Canons were founded in the twelfth century: Holy Trinity, in Christchurch Park, and SS Peter and Paul, near the docks. They provided most of the parish clergy for the town's churches, three more of which were added in the early Middle Ages. St Clement's, about 1200, shows how the port was developing: this was the parish church for a new area growing up alongside the eastern side of the quay, as trade increased. St Mary Quay and St Helen's were a little later, and the latter was possibly meant to serve a new industrial part of Ipswich.

In the reign of King John, in 1200, Ipswich obtained its first Royal Charter of Privileges. Roger Bigod, son of that Hugh whose castle had been slighted, was instrumental in procuring it from the King. In return for an increased payment, or 'farm', the townspeople of Ipswich were, by the Charter, allowed to govern themselves. They could choose their own officers, set up their own courts, and trade anywhere in England without paying tolls. They were also allowed to set up a guild merchant, a kind of society to organize and maintain standards in the trade and commerce of the town. By 1479 there were forty-four guilds in Ipswich, and the guild meetings, at the Guildhall near the Cornhill, were as important as the town government itself.

A detailed account survives of how the Charter was received and celebrated. On 29 June 1200, a crowd of people met in St Mary Tower churchyard, and chose two Bailiffs who promised to keep their office faithfully and treat both rich and poor lawfully. Four Coroners were also chosen, then the Coroners and Bailiffs appointed representatives from every parish to select twelve Portmen, to act as a kind of town council, upholding the terms of the Charter and administering justice. When these Portmen were eventually selected and appointed, another meeting was called at which they made all the spectators stretch out their hands towards a copy of the Bible, swearing to be obedient and help preserve the free customs of the town. As a reward for their services the Portmen were given the right to graze their horses on 'Portmen Marshes', where Portman Road (and the town football ground) now is.

The town seal was made and shown to the public on 12 October. On one side was a ship, emphasizing Ipswich's association with trade and the sea. On the other was a church, perhaps St Mary Tower, or St Mildred's on the Cornhill.

An Ipswich seal – the Latin inscription means 'Seal of the office of the Bailiffs of Ipswich'

In this way, Ipswich ran its own affairs from the thirteenth to the nineteenth century, except for two periods. In 1283 a mob attacked the Sheriff presiding at the County Court, and held him to ransom for two barrels of wine. Edward I, angered by such disrespect shown to this official, took the town back into his own hands and restored it only when its people, in 1291, proved their loyalty by service and additional taxation in wartime. Then in 1344 a gang of sailors took over the court of one of the King's judges and held a mock trial there. Edward III seized the borough for six months, until the people redeemed it again by paying a fine. Subsequent monarchs allowed Ipswich to buy additional rights and privileges, and confirmed those they already had.

The townspeople's ordinary daily life was very much controlled by these bailiffs, coroners, and portmen. They were particularly anxious to uphold standards of business. A miller who took in payment more than his rightful share of the corn he was grinding was set in the pillory for two hours. A man was fined for agreeing to carry out work by a certain date but failing to do so. In 1352, in the general uncertainty of the Hundred Years War, fears of invasion decided the town that it must strengthen its earthen ramparts, and for this purpose the bailiffs collected money from all goods coming in to the town: a halfpenny on every cartload of corn, twopence on each bundle of cloth, and so on. The town's principal entrances were guarded by gates at the north and west. The West Gate, overlooking the roads to London and Norwich, was the most important. It stood at the end of the present-day Westgate Street, at its junction with St Matthew's Street. Its upper storey was sometimes used as a town lock-up. The other important gate – the North Gate – stood near the site of the Town Library today. Its name is perpetuated in Northgate Street, at the head of which it stood. The site of the main entrance from the east is, curiously, still undetermined.

HOW IPSWICH MAY HAVE LOOKED IN THE MIDDLE AGES

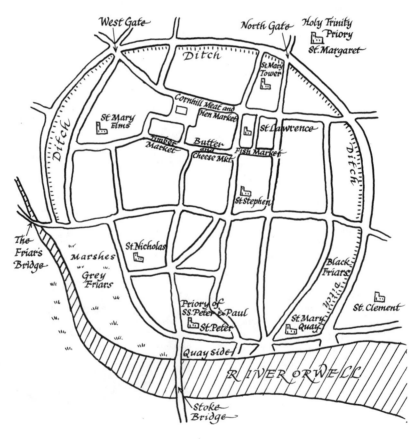

CHAPTER 9
MEDIEVAL SUFFOLK

The Domesday Survey recorded Suffolk as having about 20,000 people of all classes. Experts deduce from this that the county's actual population must have been something like 70,000. There were large manors of several hundred acres, cultivated by a number of villeins and serfs, as well as many smaller ones of 30-odd acres (12 hectares). There were a great many freemen: in most villages, freemen lived alongside villeins, with little about their way of life to distinguish one from another. Most people lived in the country, but towns developed rapidly after 1066. Dunwich, with 440 householders, was the most flourishing at the time of the Domesday Survey, even though the sea had already begun its work of destruction. Some of her prosperity came from the herring fishery. She obtained her Charter in 1200, like Ipswich. Bury, too, was becoming wealthy and more populous, with the great Abbey of St Edmund at her heart (see Chapter 10).

In the century after the Conquest, as the Normans established their control, landowners and nobles often took the law into their own hands, and built themselves castles on small earthworks. They were usually of timber, and have long since disappeared, though the mounds sometimes survive, as at Otley and Haughley. The rise of the Bigod family after the 1075 Rebellion, and their influence with William II and Henry I, made them a powerful group. For his loyalty, Roger Bigod was rewarded with the stronghold of Framlingham, but his son Hugh backed the wrong side under Henry II, and lost it again in 1157, along with his other castles at Bungay and Walton. Framlingham and Bungay were later restored to him. The King retained Walton. Eye and Haughley were already royal castles, and now Henry II, to match the Bigod power and protect the coast, built a castle at Orford (1165–73).

Its architect, Wimar the Chaplain, and Alnoth the Royal Engineer, between them made sure that Orford was the most up-to-date castle in the land. It cost the King £1,408 – nearly twice as much as he spent on two other new castles at this time, which shows how important he felt it to be. Its plan was a central keep, 90 feet (27·4 metres) tall, polygonal in shape, with three flanking towers. The surrounding earthworks were two ditches with a wall between them. When the castle was nearing completion, provisions for its garrison were collected: 700 sheep, 6 oxen, 100 'bacons', cheese, tallow, corn, salt, and fodder for 6 horses. All was ready by 1173, when Henry II's eldest son rebelled against him.

In support of this prince, the Earl of Leicester landed on the Suffolk coast with an army largely made up of foreigners. Dunwich would have none of him: a contemporary account tells how 'there was not a girl or a woman who was not carrying stones to be hurled from the palisade. . . . The Earl of Leicester went off, humiliated.' So he landed farther south, but failed to take Walton Castle. The Bigods, once again on the wrong side, sheltered him at Framlingham until their patience and hospitality were exhausted. Leicester and his troops then set off towards Bury, and were caught and defeated at the Battle of Fornham St Genevieve, a mile or two out of the town, with considerable slaughter. Forty skeletons and the rusted remains of weapons, found in 1846, probably date from this battle. Hugh Bigod hurried to make peace with the King. He was allowed, after paying a fine, to keep Bungay and his title, but 500 men (under Alnoth again) were sent to demolish Framlingham, whose walls and towers at this time were probably of wood. It was not until Hugh's son, another Roger, regained royal favour under Richard the Lionheart that the castle was rebuilt in stone, incorporating the latest ideas of fortification. With their two strongholds of Bungay and Framlingham, the power of the Bigods lasted until the beginning of the fourteenth century.

That century began with troubles. Pirates raided Dunwich and ships were attacked there. Roger Bigod instructed the county landowners to have their tenants and men in readiness to defend the coast if it became necessary. Edward II's quarrel with his Queen affected Suffolk in 1325–26. Isabella, in revolt against her husband, was expected to land here at the head of a mercenary army. Ipswich, Bawdsey, Orford, and Dunwich had to raise what forces they could to protect themselves. The Queen eventually landed near Walton and the county flocked to her as she advanced towards Bury. Lawlessness continued throughout the minority of her son, Edward III. One band of armed robbers made Stowmarket Church their headquarters, and terrorized the neighbourhood.

In the 1345 campaigns of the Hundred Years War, the ports were called on to provide ships, and troops from all over Suffolk were rallied at Ipswich. Suffolk gentlemen fought at Crécy – the names of Tollemache, Tendring, Wingfield, Barnardiston, and Huntingfield, with many others, appear in the battle-lists. Ten years later, those same names reappear in further campaigns, but with sons replacing their fathers, for in the intervening decade the Black Death had visited the county.

Hard facts and figures about the plague known as the 'Black Death' are almost non-existent. Our knowledge of its extent has to be pieced together from other records. We know, for example, that Bishop Bateman of Norwich ordained more priests (many of them boys) in seven weeks than he usually did in a whole year, to replace those who had died ministering to the sick. Records show that many parishes had a new priest in 1349–50, and sometimes more than one: Pakefield and Hark-stead both had one in May and another in June, and Whitton, outside Ipswich, had three, in March, April, and May. Sudbury's market was flourishing in 1314: there were eighty stalls that year, and this number rose to 107 in 1340. By 1361, a few years after the plague, there were only sixty-two. Perhaps the most telling evidence of all comes from the (now-vanished) village of Little Cornard, near Sudbury. When the manor court there met on 31 March 1349, it noted that three men and six women had died in the last two months, out of a total of about sixty villagers. The following month, thirteen more men and another two women had died. The court met no more until November, and it is not hard to guess why. By that time there had been thirty-six more deaths, including the priest, and thirteen families had been completely extinguished.

It is generally accepted that, over the whole country, between one-third and one-half of the people died in this epidemic. So there was naturally a labour shortage. Marginal land, such as reclaimed heathland, was the first to be abandoned, and tracts that had been made to yield crops reverted to their original state. There were fewer people to do the same amount of work. Landowners refused to pay the higher wages necessary under these new conditions of life and work, and the people were equally determined not to work for the old rates of pay when their labour was at such a premium. When the Government intervened, ordering wages to be pegged at the old level, the exasperation of a large class of the community found outlet in the Peasants' Revolt of 1381. But in Suffolk, at least, as much of that year's troubles stemmed from a desire to pay off old scores as came from genuine agricultural hardship and distress.

John Wrawe, a Sudbury chaplain, was the local leader. On 13 June, a mob under his command raided and robbed Cavendish Church. They went on, next day, to Bury, where they attacked and burned the houses of John de Cambridge, the Prior

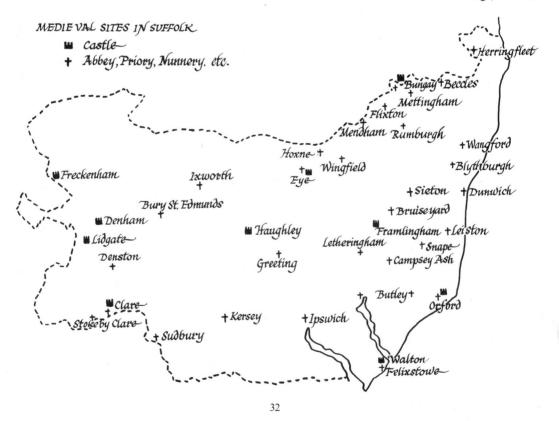

MEDIEVAL SITES IN SUFFOLK
  ♜ Castle
  ✝ Abbey, Priory, Nunnery, etc.

Herringfleet
Bungay Beccles
Mettingham
Flixton
Mendham Rumburgh
Wangford
Hoxne
Wingfield
Blythburgh
Freckenham
Ixworth
Eye
Sieton Dunwich
Bury St. Edmunds
Bruiseyard
Denham
Haughley
Framlingham Leiston
Lidgate
Letheringham Snape
Denston
Greeting
Campsey Ash
Butley
Clare
Orford
Stoke by Clare
Kersey
Ipswich
Sudbury
Walton
Felixstowe

Hadleigh's medieval bridge led into the market-place

of Bury and John de Cavendish, one of the King's officials who had been responsible for enforcing the unpopular wage restraint. He tried to escape by river but was foiled by a woman who, realizing what he meant to do, pushed the boat into midstream before he could board it. His head was hacked off and so was that of the Prior. Both heads were carried on poles to Bury, and placed over the pillory there.

In East Suffolk, troubles began in the Ipswich area on 15 June. A gang under the parson of Bucklesham looted houses in the town, as well as property at Needham Market, East Bergholt, and Stratford. They burned the manor-houses of Melton, Bawdsey, and Hollesley, destroying court-rolls and taxation records. The arrival of the Earl of Suffolk at the head of 500 men finally quelled the revolt. Severe punishments were meted out, and Wrawe himself was hanged, drawn, and quartered.

In spite of the unsettled nature of the times, Suffolk's trade and commerce increased steadily. By the end of the Middle Ages, this was the fourth richest county, and nearly a hundred towns and villages held a market, or had permission to hold one, compared with the dozen existing when 'Domesday Book' was made. Markets were the principal places for buying and selling goods in those days. Sometimes a market grew up at an important road junction. Sometimes it started, or was expanded, to serve the needs of a growing community, such as a monastery or castle, like Henry II's castle at Orford. The coming of the Normans often changed an established pattern. For example, at Clare, the pre-Conquest market-place and, therefore, presumably the major settlement, lay to the north of the church (see the map on page 34). When the Nomans built their castle, they sited it to the south, towards the river. So the market shifted, nearer to the castle approaches, occupying the open space between the church and the castle's outer bailey.

The right to hold a market was granted by the Crown to the lord of the manor, or someone of high standing, such as the Abbot of Bury. Those

33

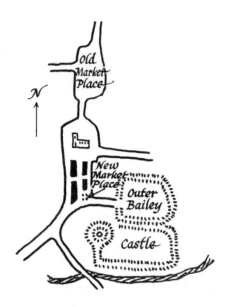

who wanted to trade at the lord's market had to pay a toll for that privilege. Most markets were held on one day – or sometimes two – each week, though a busy town might have a daily one. The Dunwich historian, writing in the eighteenth century, said: 'Formerly the markets supplied the town every day in the week, but decreased as the borough declined, to one weekly, on Saturdays.' Ipswich had two business centres. One was the common quay, where the trade of the port was carried on. Foreign merchants in the streets, and continental ships tied up alongside her wharves, must have been familiar sights in medieval Ipswich. Trade went on in food and drink, and raw materials, and as the Suffolk cloth trade prospered in the fourteenth century, the holds of outgoing ships were filled with kerseys and linsey-woolseys from the villages that made them and gave them those names.

The other commercial area was on and round the Cornhill. The great corn-market there yielded the handsome profit of £25 in 1340. The streets near by housed trade in other commodities. The name of the Butter-Market still tells us what was once sold there. The fish-market was a little farther out, near St Lawrence's Church. For hens you went to Tower Street, and for apples to Princes Street: the drapers and cloth-sellers had stalls there too. Tavern Street, still the town's main thoroughfare, used to be called 'the Cowerie': it was there that you found stalls selling meat and wine. The taverns and public-houses along its length were popular with the customers. A boy from the family who owned the tavern where the British Home Stores now stands grew up to be the father of Chaucer, author of *The Canterbury Tales*.

Market practices were carefully controlled by the bailiffs, who 'did charge and command in the king's behalf all manner of persons that intend to sell within this town . . . that they resort to the market place that is assigned and ordained for them . . . and not elsewhere'. There were rules about 'forestalling', that is intercepting and buying goods before they reached the market so as to resell them at a profit. Offenders were put in the pillory for this. Butchers who sold bad meat had it confiscated and burnt in the market-place. A woman from Shelland was robbed of four sheep on her way to market in 1325. She trailed the thief to Ipswich and accused him in public in the 'Bestesmarkat' where he had gone to sell them as his own. He was tried, found guilty, and hanged.

The other trading-centres – fairs – were held less often, perhaps once or twice a year and usually on some special occasion. Dunwich had St Leonard's Fair, held in St Leonard's Parish for three days in November, and St James's Fair, on St James's Day and the day after. In Ipswich, the May Cattle Fair, sometimes called 'St George's Fair', took place on the Cornhill and in the streets around. The profits from another fair, that of St James, went to the local leper hospital. Bury Fair, held each July, was one of the biggest in England, patronized by London merchants who came there to stock their warehouses. Its fame is demonstrated by the fact that Henry III sent William, the Royal Tailor, to Bury Fair, to buy furred robes of scarlet and black, and tunics and mantles made on the looms of Ghent and Ypres.

Henry II's castle keep at Orford

CHAPTER 10
MEDIEVAL CHURCHES AND BURY ABBEY

According to the Domesday Survey, there were about 400 churches in Suffolk, in spite of the ravages of the Danes. Most were probably simple wooden buildings; though here and there, at Gosbeck and Little Bradley, for instance, the flint frame of the small pre-Conquest nave seems to survive. Anyway, the Norman period was one of great rebuilding. With their work done, there was a lull in the thirteenth century: then the fourteenth and fifteenth centuries were an age of tremendous activity during which some parish churches – Long Melford and Southwold, for example – were almost totally rebuilt, while others were enriched and embellished with magnificent towers and other features.

In the fourteenth century, naves were widened and larger windows inserted. Where additional accommodation was needed, side aisles were added to an existing nave, or the east wall removed for lengthening the chancel. The demand for greater comfort meant that porches now began to be added to churches, usually on the south side, taking advantage of the sun's light and warmth. Such a porch sometimes had a room above it, perhaps for a priest's chamber, or to be used as the parish library or schoolroom, or – at Mendlesham – as a repository for armour and weapons. (Mendlesham still has its collection of helmets, gauntlets, and other items of armour, used by the men of the parish when they went to war.) We tend to forget that in the Middle Ages, with almost no public buildings, the church, or at least the nave of the church, was used for other purposes than worship. Courts met there, elections were held there, and for many people it was the obvious place to store valuables: anyone who stole from a church was committing sacrilege, and this was punishable by flaying alive.

The fifteenth century was the greatest period of church-building. Wealthy families, like the Lavenham clothiers, spent lavishly on reconstructing their churches on a grand scale. Some endowed chantry chapels in the churches, with rich furnishings and decorations. Church 'ales', like modern bring-and-buy sales, were sometimes organized to bring in extra funds. Cratfield held five of these in 1490. The proceeds went towards such expenses as 'peyntyng of ye image of Our Lady'. Suffolk timber provided handsome furnishings, and artists decorated the walls.

Even a small or poor parish could add an extra stage to an existing tower, but many were built, or completely rebuilt. The beautiful mixture of freestone and flint, called 'flushwork', was used to decorate the new towers, especially their parapets. A new tower at the west end of the church increased the building's length: there was usually a lofty tower-arch into the nave, and extra light from a large west window. It must have been difficult, in medieval Suffolk, to escape from the sound of bells, hung in these new towers. Many were cast locally; Bury had a flourishing foundry in the fifteenth century, but probably most of the Suffolk bells were made at Norwich. One at Sudbury has the inscription in Latin: 'Star of the sea, most holy Mary, succour us.' Another, at Stoke-by-Clare, says 'Rise in the morning, to serve God'.

Porch at St Mary's Church, Woodbridge, with Patrons' initials in flushwork

Inside the church, where there was a particularly fine roof, light was thrown on to it by an upper stage of windows above the nave, called the 'clerestory'. (When you see a clerestoried church, such as Blythburgh, those windows are an indication of something worth seeing inside.) They also lighted the rood. Nave and chancel were separated by a carved screen, its base panels painted with saints and martyrs. On top of the screen were figures of

Christ on the Cross, the Virgin and St John on either side. A narrow staircase in a near-by wall gave access to the rood, to place lights there, or to hang the veils which shrouded the figures during Lent. Roods were a particular target of the Puritans in the sixteenth and seventeenth centuries, and few remain. Eye has a fine restored one. But the rood-stairways are often still visible.

It is hard to realize that the inside of a medieval church was highly coloured, its walls painted with representations of miracles, the martyrdom of St Edmund, and so on. In an age when few could read, these paintings were a useful form of picture-teaching for parish priests. So was the Doom, usually painted above the chancel arch, behind or above the rood, where all could see it as they sat in church. It showed the Day of Judgment. Sometimes God sat in majesty, while angels round him sorted out the candidates for Heaven and Hell. The good souls, looking smug and successful, were sent up to Heaven. The bad ones were dispatched downwards, to join the demons already clawing up to claim them. The best survival of one of these Dooms in Suffolk is at Wenhaston, near Halesworth. Fortunately, it was not destroyed but merely whitewashed over. Then in the 1890s this whitewashed board was taken, during restoration-work, into the churchyard. Rain that night removed some of the whitening and the colours showed through. It is back in the church now, realistically restored, and standing in the nave, where everyone can see this strange medieval relic at close quarters.

St Edmund's tomb

The Benedictine Abbey of St Edmund at Bury was one of the greatest in the kingdom. Edmund, King of East Anglia, had been slaughtered by the Danes in 869 (see page 27). Probably in 903, or thereabouts, his remains were transferred to Beodricsworth, as Bury was called then, to a wooden church, guarded by a few priests. A century later, twenty monks following the Rule of St Benedict were installed, and Uvius consecrated as their first Abbot. Cnut granted money for a stone

(Opposite) Wingfield – staircase leading to the rood-loft

church to be built, dedicated to Christ, St Mary, and St Edmund.

The Abbey grew more and more powerful as successive kings granted additional privileges. It was exempt from the normal ecclesiastical jurisdiction, and its monks were allowed to elect their own Abbot. Edward the Confessor, in whose reign the name 'Bury St Edmunds' (that is the 'burgh of St Edmund') appears for the first time, influenced the election of Baldwin as Abbot in 1065. This remarkable Frenchman rebuilt the church on a grander scale: stone from the Northamptonshire quarries of Barnack came, on the Conqueror's orders, free of the usual tolls. A great bell was obtained to hang in the central tower. By 1095 the Abbey Church was ready to receive Edmund's body. Right up to the Dissolution of the Monasteries in the sixteenth century, pilgrims flocked to Edmund's shrine, or tomb, to ask favours or to give thanks for those granted. They included a number of the medieval kings: Henry I, Richard I, John, Henry III, Edward I, Richard II, and Henry VI all came to Bury. The last-named stayed for about four months over the winter of 1433–34. He was presented with the beautiful illuminated life of St Edmund, now in the British Museum, from which the illustration here of the Saint's shrine is taken.

Our knowledge of Bury Abbey is much increased by the *Chronicle* of one of the monks, Jocelin of Brakelond, written in the twelfth century. Jocelin was the Sacrist (the monk responsible for the church buildings) at the time of Abbot Samson. In his thirty years as Abbot, Samson paid off the Abbey's debts and added to the splendours of its church. The illustration on page 38 shows how it must have looked at this time. The great west front, 246 feet (75·7 metres) across (and still surviving, though now with houses built into its three arches) was completed in Samson's time. Its bronze doors were made by Master Hugo, perhaps the finest craftsman of that age. Pilgrims approached through what we call the 'Norman Tower', built 1120–48, which was, and still is, the belfry of the neighbouring St James's Church, now the Cathedral. As a little boy, Samson had dreamed that the Devil was trying to claim him, outside that gate, and St Edmund protected him, pulling him back. The child's story so impressed his mother that she took him, from their Norfolk home, to enter Bury Abbey as a novice, feeling that this was what the dream had intended to happen. At Bury, the boy immediately recognized the gateway as the one in his dream. Perhaps because of this, Samson always had a special feeling for St Edmund. In 1190 he raised the shrine on to a more exalted platform, behind the high altar in the church. Jocelin's *Chronicle* tells how he held the light while the coffin was opened, so that Samson could hold the Saint's hands in his own, and run his fingers through Edmund's hair.

Samson wanted to go on the Crusade but Henry II refused to allow it. He took an active part in collecting Richard the Lionheart's ransom, after that King was captured in Austria, and sold some of the Abbey plate to help raise money for it. With King John, Samson was on less good terms. When Samson died, in 1211, England, through John's obstinacy, was under the Pope's Interdict, so that no one could be buried in consecrated ground. When the Interdict was removed, in 1213, Samson was reinterred in the chapter-house of the Abbey: his grave and five more, can be seen. On St Edmund's Day 1214, the earls and barons of England met in the Abbey Church and swore to make John agree to the terms of Magna Charta.

The town of Bury benefited greatly from its association with the Abbey. Abbot Baldwin replanned the town and laid out its streets in the pattern most of them still retain. The Abbey employed a great many servants and craftsmen and provided a market for local produce. But all the same, there were many who grew to resent the Abbot's supremacy as lord of the town. Ill-feeling came to a head in 1327 in the Great Riot. In the subsequent inquiry, the Abbot accused 300 people of offences: they had beaten the Abbey's servants, broken down doors and windows, fished unlawfully in the Abbey ponds, stolen goods and cattle, and cut off the Abbey's water-supply. These disputes were finally settled in 1331, in the King's presence. The defendants were heavily fined, and made to rebuild the great Abbey gate which still stands on Angel Hill. It is significant that the new gate incorporated slit-windows, in case there was ever need to defend it against another riot by the townspeople.

In 1284 there were eighty monks and twenty-one chaplains. There were also 111 servants. Those in the Cellarer's department included the porter of the great gate, the hall steward, and many underlings. The Chamberlain had seven, including a tailor and a shoemaker. Seven more served under the Guest Master, for one of the Abbey's functions was to provide hospitality for travellers and pilgrims.

Ninety-four loaves were baked every day, in addition to those for the Abbot's Lodging, the monks' refectory, the infirmary, and the guest-house. The household servants had a daily allowance of 82 gallons (375 litres) of beer. Food at Bury would have been plain but plentiful, with treats on special days, such as the many Church festivals: pancakes for the Epiphany, apples and pears at Easter, Whitsun, Christmas, and St Edmund's Day; special round cakes called 'ringes' on the anniversary of Richard I's accession.

The Abbey's great collection of more than 2,000 books was famous. In 1430 a special library was built to house them, and regulations were drawn up for their use. Some of these volumes survived the break-up of the Abbey. One especially fine one, called the 'Bury Bible', of the time of Abbot Samson, may, like those bronze doors, have been the work of Master Hugo. It is now in the Library of Corpus Christi College at Cambridge.

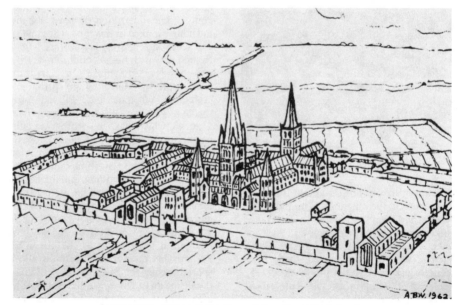

St Edmund's Abbey at the time of Jocelin of Brakelond

CHAPTER 11
SUFFOLK'S CLOTH TRADE: THE SPRINGS OF LAVENHAM

It seems strange, in the twentieth century, to think that throughout the Middle Ages south-west Suffolk was an industrial area. The little towns and villages there – Lavenham, Long Melford, Hadleigh, Kersey, and many more – were all centres of the cloth-making trade, in which East Anglia rivalled Yorkshire and the Cotswolds. Almost all of them lay on those streams, the Stour and its tributaries, whose fast-flowing water provided the power for the fulling-mills. The fifteenth-century prosperity of the whole region is reflected in its splendid churches, rebuilt and enriched with the money of wealthy clothiers, like Thomas Spring of Lavenham.

For centuries, English cloth was the principal material for making clothes. In the Early Norman period, wool was sent abroad for weaving, but later, with royal encouragement, cloth-making began at home. The heads of this industry were some of the richest men in the land, owning manors, gaining titles, marrying their children into the aristocracy.

Most of the wool was grown locally, and June was shearing-time in Suffolk. Important clothiers like the Springs who owned manors and farms probably grew their own wool. Then they put it out among the village people to be processed and made into cloth. Even children were useful here: they could pick the dirt out of the shorn fleeces, and separate the strands of wool. Some charitable institutions made use of their inmates in this way. At Christ's Hospital, Ipswich, children were set to card and spin wool from their earliest years. Women and girls did most of the spinning, working at home. Before the spinning-wheel was invented, in 1530, they used a distaff, portable and easy, which could be tucked under one arm. It must have been a temptation to keep back a little of what you spun for your own use, but the penalties for pilfering were discouraging: the pillory and the ducking-chair. Perhaps it was to remove this temptation that one thoughtful master left, in his will, enough wool for each of his spinners to make themselves a smock.

The clothiers sent riders round to collect the spun yarn and deliver it to the weavers, usually men, and again working at home. The looms were simple wooden frames. The operator pushed a bar down to press the wefts close together. One Lavenham clothier bequeathed to his wife his 'best payre of loomys' and to his servant his 'olde loome'.

The woven cloth had to be dyed and fulled. Nearly every clothier had his own dye-house, with vats and tubs. The usual colours were blues, greens, and purples. Woad for colouring came from Spain:

it was crushed, mixed with water, and left to ferment before the cloth was dipped. 'Cutchenel' was also used, to produce red. Then came fulling, when the lengths of cloth were beaten or scoured in water, to remove the natural grease. They were hung to dry on 'tenters', large wooden frames. In Lavenham, one tenter-yard lay between the church and the house of Thomas Sexton, a clothier. The expression we still use, about being 'on tenterhooks' (that is kept in suspense), is a survival from this practice. It was tempting, at this stage, to stretch the lengths of cloth, making them seem longer than they really were, and the guilds, which controlled trade, had strict regulations about this, wanting to maintain the high reputation held abroad by English cloth.

Sometimes the cloth was bought immediately by London merchants, to be 'finished' elsewhere. But more usually it was finished at home: loose ends were snipped off, and the fluffy knap of the cloth brushed up with a prickly teasle. Teasles still grow in the Suffolk lanes and must be the descendants of those medieval ones.

A Government official, the 'ulnager', inspected all cloth, measuring it and examining it for flaws before

Lavenham Church

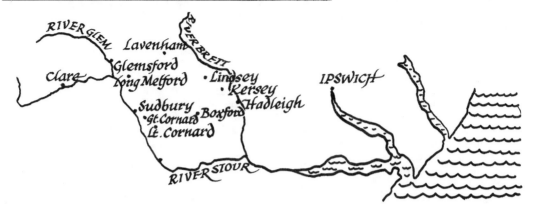

sealing it as perfect. (An ulnager's seal was found at Hadleigh, early this century.) Then packhorses, or great carts called 'wains', took the cloth to Ipswich for export, or carried it overland to London, or to the great fairs at Bury, and Stourbridge, near Cambridge.

There were three guilds in Lavenham, all connected with the cloth trade. They fixed wages, regulated hours of work, and supervised the quality of the finished cloth. Members of a guild and their families were given help if they were ill, or in other kinds of trouble. The present early-sixteenth-century Guildhall was the meeting-place of the Guild of Corpus Christi, and the Feast of Corpus Christi was one of the town's great days. It began with a procession round the town, led by the priest and the Master of the Guild, followed by the other members. There was a special service in church, and afterwards a feast in the Guildhall. Business meetings used to be held there too, with members meeting to discuss the problems of their trade, or settle disputes among themselves.

The town of Lavenham had a great many clothiers – thirty-four of them in 1522 – but the

The Guildhall at Lavenham

Spring family were the richest. The first Thomas Spring died in 1440, leaving money to the parish church. His son, Thomas Spring II, died in 1486. He left money to his workers, and some towards road repairs in the neighbourhood. Several clothiers did this: perhaps they recalled times when their workpeople had to remain idle because the roads were too bad to bring in fresh supplies of materials. John Hunt left £15 for mending the highway between Lavenham and Long Melford and, in his will, said that it was 'to be done immediately after my decease'. Thomas Spring II's most lasting bequest was £200 towards the building of the great church tower. His merchant's mark, a kind of trade badge, with his initials 'TS', and an elaborate 'L' for Lavenham, appear in its stonework, along with a star, part of the badge of the De Vere family, earls of Oxford and lords of the manor at Lavenham. There is a memorial brass of Spring near his tomb in the church. He, his wife, their four sons and six daughters, are rising from their grave on Judgment Day.

Thomas Spring III – depicted on his father's memorial brass

Thomas Spring III may have learnt the trade from his father, or during an apprenticeship to another clothier. When he became head of the family business, he could shear, weave, dye, and full as well as any of his workers. So successful in business was he that, after his death in 1523, his widow was the second richest person in Suffolk, even after paying her taxes. The eldest son gave up trade, became a country gentleman, and was eventually knighted. One daughter married into the Jermyn family of Rushbrooke Hall, near Bury.

Lavenham owed its importance in the late fifteenth century to this Thomas Spring III. He owned land all over East Anglia, and several houses in Lavenham itself, besides his own 'hed house' which may have been in the Market-Place. There are still many houses in Lavenham which look much as the Spring house would have done. Thomas Spring III's will gives us some idea of the contents, for he left his 'plate, ornaments and implements of household, as bedding, napyre, hangings, brasse, pewter, and all other hostilments of house' to be shared between his wife and his eldest son. He also left money so that in all the places where he owned land (more than a hundred villages), 'priests, clerks and pour folks' should pray for his soul. Most important for posterity, he left £200 to finish building the church tower. Alice, his widow, built the Spring Chapel in the church, with her husband's initials in its carved roof.

By 1523 when Thomas Spring III died, Lavenham's greatest days were over. For one thing, there was increasing competition from the 'New Draperies', the popular lighter fabrics which were being produced abroad. And Cardinal Wolsey, needing money for his war against France, imposed a heavy tax on everybody worth over £40. The Babergh district, where the clothing towns lay, paid £615, one-sixth of the whole Suffolk total, and of this Lavenham itself contributed £180. When Wolsey called for a second payment, the clothiers saw that it was not in their interests to employ so many workers, and began to dismiss them, causing hardship in an age when there was no State help for the unemployed. Shakespeare, in his play *Henry VIII*, makes reference to the problem:

> . . . For upon these taxations
> The clothiers all, not able to maintain
> The many to them 'longing, have put off
> The spinsters, carders, fullers, weavers . . .

And part of a poem of this time, written by a Norfolk man, John Skelton, says:

> Good Springe of Lanam
> Must count what became
> Of his clothe making
> Though his purse wax dull
> He must tax for his wul . . .
> He must paye agayne
> A thousand or twayn
> Of his gold in store.

The newly hung bells in Lavenham's vast church tower were rung in 1525, not to call the people to worship, but to summon 4,000 of them to protest at the effects of unemployment.

CHAPTER 12
THE REFORMATION IN SUFFOLK

Chapters 10 and 11 showed something of the wealth and power of the Church. In the fifteenth century, this at last began to be questioned and criticized by such writers and preachers as Wycliffe in England and Luther and Calvin on the Continent, who urged that priests and monks were not as holy as they should be. Christ, they said, had been poor, but the Church had great possessions, and some men became monks to enjoy an easy life. There were some serious abuses, where priests held more than one living, and failed to perform their prescribed duties. A good deal of money went each year from England to the Pope in Rome.

Those who questioned, or protested about, the established Church were called 'Protestants'. Suffolk, so close to Europe where most of the new ideas and the books expounding them originated, became a centre of the reforming zeal which eventually changed the system and put the King, not the Pope, at the head of the Church in England. The Waveney Valley, quite early in the fifteenth century, produced a batch of critics who were charged with such offences as saying that the Pope was anti-Christ. They were imprisoned at Framlingham, where most of them recanted under the threat of dreadful penalties. In 1431, Nicholas Conon of Eye hid behind a pillar in church on Easter Day, and mocked the priest as he stood at the altar. When charged, he boasted about what he had done, and said he had done it well. Bishop Nykke of Norwich was active in chasing these 'heretics', the name given to people who departed from the accepted ways. There are records of some being branded with hot irons and, in 1515, after troubles at Bungay, where men 'arrayed as rioters' caused a disturbance in church, a formal complaint was sent to Cardinal Wolsey himself.

Wolsey was a native of Ipswich, born about 1472–73, the son of a butcher and inn-keeper in the Parish of St Nicholas. In later life, his enemies never let him forget his humble origins. He was probably educated in Ipswich before going, as a boy, to Oxford. He was clever and ambitious: Henry VII, whose Chaplain he became, soon recognized his abilities, and Henry VIII continued the royal patronage. In a short time, Wolsey became Bishop of Lincoln, then Archbishop of York. He was made a Cardinal in 1515, and clearly had visions of becoming Pope.

In June 1528, work began on 'The Cardinal College of St Mary's in Ipswich', Wolsey's magnificent gift to the town where he was born. The

Cardinal Wolsey

site of St Peter's Priory, near the river, was seized and used for the college buildings, and St Peter's Church itself was absorbed into them. Several small monasteries, including those at Snape and Felixstowe, were suppressed by the Cardinal, so that their endowments and property could be appropriated for the new college. Within three months enough of the buildings were ready for the first pupils to take up residence. A grand opening ceremony was planned for 6 September 1528. It would be Wolsey's finest moment, his answer to the town which, years before, had punished his father several times for transgressing its trade regulations. It was a pity for Wolsey that the day was wet, and the procession which should have gone through the town had to be confined to the college precincts. The day's celebrations ended with a venison banquet, also provided by the Cardinal.

Throughout 1528–29 the college buildings continued to rise. Shiploads of Normandy stone, and timber, and lead for the roofs, arrived at the

Ipswich quays. All was brought to the college site, where the schoolmaster was soon complaining that, because of the mess, there was scarcely room enough for the scholars to work. By July 1529 much of the building was finished, but by then Wolsey had fallen from the royal favour. Henry VIII determined to divorce his first wife, Catherine of Aragon, and marry Anne Boleyn. The Pope would not allow it, nor could Wolsey persuade him. It had been his last hope of ingratiating himself again with the King: when he failed, Henry had no further use for him. Accusations were made against him, and he was summoned to London, and the Tower. On his way there, in November 1530, Wolsey became ill and died at Leicester Abbey. The King ordered the Ipswich college to be dissolved. The building materials were shipped back to London, to be used in the royal works at Westminster. Only a gateway, called 'Wolsey's Gate', still stands there, with a commemorative tablet near by, and the eroded arms of Henry VIII above its door.

A nineteenth-century photograph of Wolsey's Gate

Reforming ideas continued to gain ground, in spite of severe punishments for anyone found preaching them. They even filtered into some of the monasteries. The Church did its best to reclaim the waverers. Richard Bayfield, Chamberlain of Bury Abbey, 'was cast into the prison of his house, there sore whipped, with a gagge in his mouth', for using Tyndale's version of the Bible instead of the Latin Vulgate. He was eventually burnt at the stake. William Leiton, a former monk of Eye Priory, died 'for speaking against a certain Idoll which was accustomed to be carried about the Processions'.

Henry VIII's solution to the problem of the royal divorce was, finally, to make a break with the Catholic Church, and establish his own, the Church of England, with himself at its head. He was then able to grant his own divorce, and dismantle the fabric of a thousand years of Catholicism. His new adviser, Thomas Cromwell, urged him to get rid of the monasteries. There was a precedent in Wolsey's seizure of small religious houses to get funds for the Ipswich college. The monasteries were rich, and were thought by many to be full of lazy and hypocritical monks. This was perhaps too sweeping a generalization, but there were certainly some places where such accusations were justifiable. When Butley Priory, one of the richest in Suffolk, was examined by the Bishop in 1532, a flood of grievances poured into his ears. The monks complained of the coldness of their refectory, and the lack of salt fish from their meals. No proper accounts had been kept for thirty years. The Sub-Prior had taken for his own use some pewter mugs which belonged to the infirmary. A young servant was eating most of the fresh vegetables which should have gone to the monks. Blythburgh Priory was in debt, and one monk there complained that the Prior was too lenient to his favourites and too cruel and severe to those he disliked. Part of the church of Woodbridge Priory was dilapidated, and the Prior had spent too much money on making a water-mill. The nunneries were no better. A nun at Campsey Priory said they had had to eat a bullock which would have died from disease had it not been slaughtered for the table. The strongest criticisms came from Bury Abbey. The royal officials sent there reported back to Cromwell about lax discipline and the abundance of so-called 'holy relics' which, pilgrims had believed for years, could work miracles: 'As for the abbot, we found that he delited much in playing at dice and cards.... Amongst the relics we found much vanitie and superstition, as the coals that St. Laurence was toasted withal, the paring of St. Edmund's nails ... pieces of the holye cross able to make a whole cross of....' The report referred also to the abbey's great wealth: '... we found a rich shrine which was very cumbrous to deface. We have taken in the said monastery in gold and silver 5,000 marks and over, as well as a rich cross with emeralds, also divers and sundry stones of great value. ...'

Between 1536 and 1539, Suffolk was swept clean of all the religious Orders, and the change must have been felt keenly by many people who had looked to the monasteries for charity and

employment. Occasionally, pensions were paid to the dispossessed monks: the Abbot of Leiston got £20 a year, twenty-six Bury monks got £177 between them. But such outgoings were negligible compared with the King's great gains. From Bury alone he took 1,553 oz (44 kg) of gold, 6,853 oz (195 kg) of silver plate, and was able to sell the bells and lead from the roofs for 4,500 marks (£3,000). He also took, and either sold or gave away, thousands of acres of monastic land.

In 1547, in the closing months of Henry VIII's reign, Commissioners were appointed to compile inventories of church goods: the first step to their being snatched by the Crown. Several parishes felt, with some justification, that if their treasures must go, then they, rather than the King, should keep the proceeds. The new ideas of Protestantism had taken hold quickly in Suffolk, and it was not much hardship to part with what many churchwardens and parishioners considered to be unnecessary decorations. Aldeburgh realized £40 by selling a cross, chalice, and candlesticks, and used the money to buy 'powder and shot for the realm'. Barking got £54 for similar church plate, and bought a new organ with the money. Beccles sold some of its silver for £59 which it spent 'for the edifyinge, byldynge and fynyshinge of our steeple', that handsome detached bell-tower which still presides over the town.

Under Edward VI (1547–53), Parliament's Act of Suppression abolished chantries and chantry-priests. The Commissioners for Suffolk had the courage to point out the hardship this would inflict on some places where (as at Lavenham and Woodbridge) the chantry-priest helped the one curate to administer the whole parish, or where he provided such schooling as the children had.

The reign of Mary (1553–58), daughter of Henry VIII and Catherine of Aragon, was a disastrous one. She came to the throne on a wave of popularity. Thousands rallied to join her at Framlingham Castle, the home of the Howards, Dukes of Norfolk and the leading Catholic family in the land, whose splendid tombs stand in the church. From there they followed her to London, to claim her throne from the unfortunate Lady Jane Grey, Queen for only a few days. But Mary was uncompromisingly Roman Catholic and was determined to restore that faith throughout her kingdom, undoing the work of her father and brother. In the short reign which earned her the name of 'Bloody Mary', Protestants were burnt at the stake for refusing to abandon the new faith and return to the old. Three men were burnt at Beccles in 1556 and two more at Debenham. A number from the countryside round Ipswich were taken there, to die on the Cornhill, including several women. They were fastened to the post with irons and surrounded by broom and faggots. Atrocities like these encouraged Protestant feeling, already strong in Suffolk. A nineteenth-century memorial to the Marian martyrs stands in Christchurch Park in Ipswich. On Aldham Common, just outside Hadleigh, a rough contemporary stone with a moving inscription marks the spot where, in 1553, Dr Rowland Taylor, the priest, was burnt for refusing to abandon his beliefs.

The Dissolution of the Monasteries: ruins of Leiston Abbey
(Opposite) The bell-tower of St Michael's Church, Beccles

CHAPTER 13
SUFFOLK AND THE CIVIL WAR

The troubles associated with Puritanism and the Civil War of the seventeenth century really began in the sixteenth. As early as 1561, Elizabeth, at Ipswich on a royal progress, complained of the clergy's refusal to wear the surplice, and at the number of married clergy she found. Ipswich's Puritanism was soon well known. The borough provided scholarly preachers to preach long sermons, and business came to a halt on Wednesdays and Fridays while the townspeople listened. The most famous of these men, Samuel Ward, a native of Haverhill, received £180 a year. His popularity and persuasiveness won him the name 'silver-tongued'. and he was Town Preacher from 1603 to 1635, until Archbishop Laud, the great enemy of Puritanism, displaced him. Bishop Corbett of Norwich, with Laud's encouragement, was also an enemy of all Nonconformity and boasted that he had made 'two wandering preachers run out of his diocese'. In spite of this, he felt bound to add, 'lecturers abound in Suffolk'.

It was partly this harassment and indirect persecution that drove a number of Suffolk men overseas to America in the early part of the century, but the county's declining prosperity was the principal cause. There was both agricultural and industrial distress: 'New Draperies' (see Chapter 11), introduced from abroad, were replacing the established cloth-manufacture. Coastal defences were being neglected, and Suffolk ships hardly dared venture from port for fear of pirates. Charles I's demands for ship-money were met grudgingly or not at all. Such problems, added to the ecclesiastical ones, were bound to make men restless. Timothy Dalton, Parson of Woolverstone, was one of those who urged emigration. Cargo ships from Ipswich and Great Yarmouth were converted to carry passengers, and several left the quaysides in the 1630s, carrying Suffolk men and women to the New World. One, John Winthrop of Groton, near Sudbury, became Governor of Massachusetts. A number of places in the United States of America have East Anglian names, indicating the origins of those who founded them.

Bishop Wren of Norwich introduced High Church practices into his diocese and encouraged Sunday recreation. This angered Puritans more. William Prynne published a pamphlet, *Newes from Ipswich*, which was specially directed at the Bishop. For this, the Court of Star Chamber ordered him to be imprisoned, and branded 'SL' (seditious libeller) on both cheeks.

(Opposite) Kedington Church – Barnardiston monuments

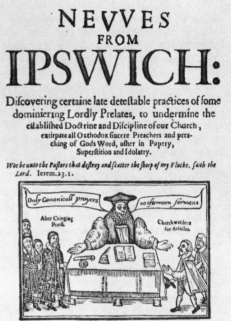

By 1641, it was fairly clear that England was heading towards a civil war. That year the Ipswich Bailiffs (chief magistrates) complained to the House of Commons about their town's sufferings through 'the unhappy misunderstanding between King and Parliament'. After Archbishop Laud's fall from power, the Puritan rulers of the town were freed from any control by a bishop. They introduced strict rules for Sunday behaviour: there must be no 'sporting or playinge at any games, walkinge at the Key, in the feildes, or . . . unnecessary roweinge in boates . . .'. Masters and parents were instructed not to let their apprentices and children 'bee playeinge and idleinge in the streetes upon the Lord's Day'.

In spite of an optimistic, conciliatory statement from the Court, in 1640, about 'his majesty having ever had a very good opinion of the love and duty of that county', Suffolk supported Parliament overwhelmingly. It is easy to exaggerate anti-Royalist feeling: at Bury, Aldeburgh, and Lowestoft, for example, there was strong Royalist support all through the Civil War and Commonwealth. But the county had only seventy-five Royalist families, compared with – for instance – 500 in Kent. The principal families who dominated affairs had been building up and consolidating their influence for three generations, and all were Puritans: the Bacons, Norths, Bedingfields, and Barnardistons. The Barnardistons, of Kedington, where their funeral monuments line the church, were the county's unquestioned leaders. Letters from Parliament were invariably addressed to 'Sir Nathaniel Barnardiston and the rest of the Committees of Suffolk.' With an annual income of £4,000, he was easily the richest man in Suffolk. A contemporary told how 'he permitted no known profane person to stand before him or wait upon him', and how in his house 'were dayly offered up the spiritual sacrifices of reading the word, and prayer, morning and evening, of singing psalmes constantly after every meal, before a servant did rise from the table'.

In his book, *Suffolk and the Great Rebellion*, Professor Alan Everitt has shown how these great Puritan families had already for many years formed a committee of the gentry in everything but name, and when a County Committee was needed in 1642, at the start of the Civil War, it was already there. It is even a tempting possibility that Parliament may have borrowed its idea of governing England by committee from this Suffolk example, which appeared to work so well. The members raised money to pay troops, and arranged billets for them, at local inns and at 'Goodwife Glover's' at Bury. The Bury carriers were employed as troop transports, the surgeons of Ipswich and Bury were busy with the 'lame and maymed'. Royalist property was confiscated, to produce extra income. The Committee kept its accounts carefully: a carpenter was paid for making a special box to keep them in, 'that this County may receive satisfaction that the moneys raysed upon them hath been imployed for their own defence'.

Suffolk saw little of the action of the war. There were local riots, at Long Melford and Stoke-by-Nayland, where enthusiastic supporters of Parliament attacked the houses and property of Royalists. In 1642, Ipswich sent to Colchester seeking advice about defences, and agreed to spend money on a hundred muskets and six barrels of powder. In July 1643, William Cage, one of the two Ipswich Members of Parliament, wrote the Bailiffs a sharp reminder that their defences needed some reorganization: 'You know that yor ditches about towne ar muche decaied and troden down and horse waies made to ride up and downe upon them and I feare they are muche digged downe where men have private yards against them. I thincke it might be a good worke to gett them made up in a good sorte, the wch I thincke might be done by invitinge the severale parishes two or three in a daie to come

some one daie and some another daie to worke and repaire the same to beginne at the ende next the washe lane and so to the old barre gates. . . .'

Ten days after this letter, and presumably as a result of it, orders were issued for fortifications round the town, fifty or so wheelbarrows being provided to help with the work. A gate was put up near the Friars' Bridge, in St Nicholas's Parish, and the key kept at a 'little howse' near by. A man was paid to keep watch on Felixstowe Beacon. This seems to be all that was thought necessary until June 1648, when Colchester was under siege. Then a stronger watch was ordered to be kept, and the Constable was to have 'three or fowre musketts goe with him'. Sailors then in the town were made to do extra guard duties (paid out of voluntary contributions) and, for additional protection, 'as many of the turne pikes as will turne bee shut upp every night'. Colchester surrendered in August, and the anxiety was over.

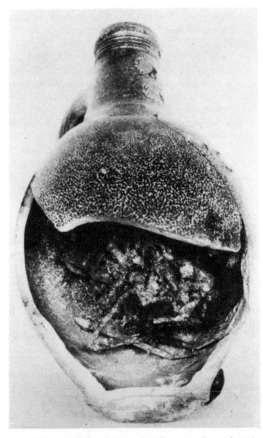

A bottle containing hair and nails was often placed under a floor as a counter-charm against witchcraft

There were, inevitably, disagreeable aspects of the strict Puritan administration. In 1645, eighteen 'witches' were tried and executed at Bury, for bewitching corn, cattle, and people. An old parson from Brandeston confessed 'that he bewitched a ship neere Harwidge'. At the height of this persecution, Matthew Hopkins, as Witchfinder-General, toured the eastern counties to discover more witches. The accounts of Aldeburgh contain the entries: 'Paid for diett and wyne when Mr. Hopkins was in Towne and for charges for the witches £4 7s.', and 'Mr. Hopkins for giving evidence against witches in the Jail, £2.' Also, Parliament decided to purge churches of what they called 'scandalous pictures' and all the ornaments which Puritans considered not merely superfluous but positively Popish such as memorial brasses, and images of the saints, painted, carved, or in stained glass. William Dowsing, born at Laxfield near Framlingham in 1596, was appointed Parliamentary Visitor of the Suffolk Churches. He kept a journal of his crusade of destruction in Suffolk in 1644, when he wantonly destroyed much of the legacy of the Middle Ages in many of our parish churches. 'Superstitious pictures', or stained-glass windows, were his favourite target. At Stoke-by-Nayland he recorded: 'We brake down an 100 superstitious pictures.' At Clare: 'We brake down 1000 Pictures superstitious', and then, with obvious pride, 'I brake down 200.' The eleven churches of Ipswich took him two days. St Matthew's lost '3 Angels with Stars on their breasts' and St Peter's a 'Crown of Thorns' as well as other items. His own birthplace, Laxfield, was treated especially thoroughly, losing 'many superstitious Inscriptions in Brass.... An eagle, and a Lion, with wings, for 2 of the Evangelists.' In Suffolk churches today, where you see defaced figures round a font, brasses prised from their matrixes, and jumbles of coloured glass fragments in the top light of an otherwise plain window, you are almost certainly looking at victims of the Puritan triumph.

Disillusion with the rule of Parliament increased throughout the 1650s. Wars against Holland and Spain interfered with trade, affecting Suffolk's prosperity even more. Nobody volunteered now for the Navy, and men had to be 'pressed' to serve. A Press Officer's report of 1652, sent to the Navy Commissioners, said: '... men are very scarse.... I purpose this night to presse what men wee can finde att Woodbridge, Orfford and Aldeburgh.... There are several villages that I am informed of that if I goe there I shall finde a great menny fishermen that wilbe very serviceable.' Another report four years later said: '... they due so hide themselfes in privat houses that we cannot find them'. Royalist feeling remained as an underground movement, emerging in 1660 when, at the Restoration, Ipswich prepared to welcome Charles II with 'fyve or six great guns provided readie att the Common Key to discharge att the same time', and sent 'twoe hundred pownds in gold and a cup of gold' to the King 'as a gift from this towne in token of our dutie and allegance'. In this county of such strong Puritan sympathies, a surprising number of parishes placed the new King's royal arms in their churches. Perhaps the finest example hangs still in the great church of St Margaret in Ipswich, the county town.

Blythburgh Church font, a victim of the iconoclast, William Dowsing

CHAPTER 14
THE AGE OF COACHES AND CANALS

Tollhouse and turnpike. The signpost points to Woodbridge, but look at those hills

In his *Tour Through the Eastern Counties* of 1724, Daniel Defoe noted enthusiastically that one of the many attractions of Ipswich was the 'easy passage to London . . . the coach going through to London in a day'. The eighteenth century was an age of improvements in communications, and these had their effect on the social and economic pattern of the county.

The principal reason for the bad state of the roads before this was the absence of a road authority, such as we have today, to maintain them. Responsibility for repairing a highway fell on those parishes through which it passed. The duty was easily evaded, and, when performed at all, was always inadequate. In the seventeenth century, tolls, which had long been payable for crossing certain bridges and ferries, were extended to some of the roads in the Home Counties. Because people were inclined to race by without stopping to pay, a law of 1695 gave local authorities the power to block the road with a turnpike: a barrier of pikes, or spikes fixed to a pole. When the requisite toll was paid, the pole was moved aside to clear the road. The eighteenth century adopted the system. Groups of local gentry formed Turnpike Trusts and obtained special Acts of Parliament to allow them to construct and maintain a stretch of road. Then, to get their money back, they put a barrier across the road and charged a toll for using it. Ordinary gates

which were simpler soon replaced the actual turnpikes, though the name survived.

Turnpike Trusts usually put up houses by their gates, and employed keepers whose job it was to collect the toll, issue tickets, and open the gates. The house was sometimes shaped so that its windows commanded views of the approach roads: the keeper could be on the look-out for traffic, and be outside, ready to open the gate with as little delay as possible. A pretty flint toll-cottage still stands at Darsham, where the A12 is joined by the road from Halesworth.

One of the earliest Turnpike Acts was that passed in 1711, to improve the roads west of Ipswich, through Claydon and Stowmarket, which, it stated, 'for many years past have been so very ruinous deep and full of holes that the same are become dangerous'. It went on to stipulate that the Trustees should 'cause to be erected one or more toll-houses . . .'. Coaches using this road were to pay 1s (5p).

Even on the turnpikes, travel was slow, and hardly comfortable. The Great Yarmouth to London coach through Ipswich, in 1743, was 'a clumsy heavy-looking thing of leather, nailed on a stout wooden frame, and fitted behind with a large wicker basket for the conveyance of luggage and the poorer class of traveller'. In 1762 it still took ten hours to get from Ipswich to London, and cost 3d

An eighteenth-century road-wagon carved on its driver's tombstone

(just over 1p) a mile. Passengers were allowed up to 18 lb (8·2 kg) of luggage, but had to pay for it. This coach, unlike most, carried no outside passengers and was described as being 'hung upon steel' for better springing.

Because travel was so expensive, at a time when a farm-labourer was fortunate if he earned 10s (50p) a week, people only travelled if they really had to, and not, as we do, for pleasure. Apart from the fare itself, there were meals to be bought, ostlers and drivers to be tipped, and – if it was a long journey – overnight accommodation at one of the coaching inns. A German traveller observed that the farther you went from London, the worse the standards of these inns became: dirty rooms, poor-quality food, uncivil servants, and – of course – higher charges. Woodbridge Crown, Beccles King's Head, Stowmarket Fox, and many smaller houses were all staging-posts in the coaching age. At Ipswich's Great White Horse, and Hadleigh's White Lion, you can still see how what was once a courtyard within the premises, into which the coach could pull to disgorge its passengers, has been roofed in to make a large room.

So it is surprising to find a young Frenchman, François de la Rochefoucauld, staying in Suffolk in 1784, expressing astonishment at the number of travellers always to be met with on the roads. In Bury alone, he noted, there were '125 horses available in the town for the service of post-chaises and diligences.... Over and above this large number you may reckon at least fifty hacks let out either as saddle-horses or for cabriolets.' He added that it was 'quite a simple matter to go from one place to another, and, what is more, to go in comfort'. His Suffolk host, Arthur Young (Chapter 2), would hardly have agreed with him: he said the road between Sudbury and Bury was one of the worst in the kingdom, and he had travelled extensively. However, improvements continued so that by 1797 Arthur Young was himself boasting that the roads were good in every part of the county. 'The improvements in this respect in the last twenty years are almost inconceivable,' he said.

The Royal Mail coaches were the fastest, with an average speed of 6–8 miles (9–13 kilometres) an hour. Stage-coaches, so called because their journeys were planned in stages between inns where horses could be changed and passengers refreshed, took a little longer. The expression 'slow coach' still used to describe someone who does not hurry himself is probably taken from one of these stopping coaches, used by people who were making a shorter journey than usual. The *Lord Nelson*, in 1807, left Great Yarmouth at 8 a.m., called at Lowestoft at 9.30, Wrentham at 11, Wangford at 11.30, Yoxford at 1 p.m., Saxmundham at 1.30, Wickham Market at 3, Woodbridge at 3.30, and reached Ipswich at 5. On a similar coach, going from Bury to London, the essayist Charles Lamb suffered boredom when he had to travel with 'one of those troublesome fellow-passengers in a stage-coach, that is called a well-informed man'. There was no way of escaping the conversation. Slowest, and cheapest, of all were the great lumbering stage-wagons, with wide wheels, jogging along at 2 miles (3 kilometres) an hour. The driver of one, buried in Palgrave churchyard, has the wagon carved on his tombstone there together with a moving little verse (see illustration on this page).

A coaching letter (see page 52)

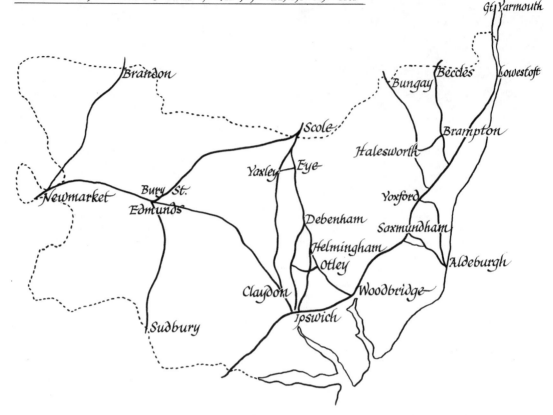

By 1829, Suffolk had 278 miles of turnpike roads, to Norfolk's 271 and Essex's 249. The first county directory, published in 1844, praised the excellence of these roads though it admitted that 'many of the bye-lanes are narrow and mirey'. There were by this time fourteen Turnpike Trusts. Thirteen of them had their roads in good repair, the other in tolerable repair. Many of the records of the Trusts survive, with details of their charges, instructions to the surveyors they employed, and complaints from toll-keepers. A letter about certain coaches being exempt from tolls on the Ipswich to Great Yarmouth Turnpike is shown on page 51. The two coaches named ran from Haxell's Office in Lower Brook Street, Ipswich. The *Shannon* went to Halesworth, and the *Retaliator* to Woodbridge. According to the same directory, it was one of 'more than twelve conveyances' which served that town 'between the hours of six in the morning and twelve at noon; and persons may travel from Woodbridge to London in five hours for 10s [50p] instead of

paying three times that amount and being thirteen hours on the road' as had been the case half a century earlier.

The general improvement in communications at this time extended to waterways. Suffolk is crossed by a series of navigable rivers (see Chapter 3) and in the seventeenth and eighteenth centuries most of them were 'improved', with locks being built to regulate the water, making it possible to ship goods farther and farther inland. The first to be so treated was the Waveney, in 1670, and Beccles and Bungay reaped the benefit. A popular saying of the time was that you could go to Bungay 'to get new-bottomed', meaning that someone who had failed in business could make a fresh start there and make a success of things. Much of Bury's eighteenth-century prosperity dated from 1698, when the River Lark was made navigable as far as the town. It meant that Bury then was linked with the River Ouse and the port of King's Lynn. Goods could be transported much more cheaply by water. Coal, especially, was drastically reduced in price, and the Lark was sometimes called the 'coal river'.

Sudbury, too, got its coal at cut-price rates after improvements in 1705. Defoe, in 1724, referred to the Stour as 'a river which parts the counties of Suffolk and Essex and which is within these few years made navigable to this town'. Some 12,000 tons (12,192 tonnes) of coal came each year to Sudbury from Manningtree along the Stour Navigation. Investors with money in the company got dividends of 14 per cent in 1835 and 30 per cent in 1846. Horses towing the barges crossed the river by jumping on to their own boats, thirty-three times. Constable's painting *The Leaping Horse* shows one of them doing it.

A proposal to make the Gipping navigable was opposed at first by Ipswich, who feared that Stowmarket would steal her trade. But it was authorized in 1790, completed in 1793, and cut the cost of getting goods between the two towns by half: very important for farmers in that agricultural region. By 1855, Stowmarket had doubled its population and, according to a directory of that year, had 'a considerable traffic in corn, malt, coal, etc., being nearly in the centre of the county and there being no other navigation within the distance of many miles'. It went on to add that the canal was 'a great ornament to the town', with an agreeable walk along the towing-path.

By the time that her road and river systems were providing the kind of services that Suffolk needed, both were doomed. They were among the first victims of the Railway Age, with which neither of them could hope to compete.

The Stowmarket end of the Gipping Navigation

CHAPTER 15
THE COMING OF THE RAILWAY

Celebrations at Bury mark the opening of the railway to Ipswich in 1846

The Railway Age really began for Suffolk on 11 June 1846. At precisely 10.25 that morning, two little engines, the *Ipswich* and the *Colchester*, pulling thirteen carriages, steamed out of Ipswich, heading south, while a brass band played 'God Save the Queen'. The Mayor had asked for the day to be kept as a public holiday and his request 'was obeyed to the letter, much to the delight of the whole population'. The little station at the southern end of Stoke Hill (the name Station Street still survives) was decorated with flowers and flags, and 600 ladies sat in a beflagged grandstand to watch the train leave.

All the way to Colchester the celebrations were kept up, and labourers ran across the fields to wave their handkerchiefs. The train halted at Bentley to receive congratulatory addresses from the neighbouring villages. At Colchester the Ipswich party was joined by a group of railway directors and engineers from London, and they all returned to Ipswich for a day's entertainment which included an excursion on the steamer *River Queen*, a balloon ascent, a firework display, and the inevitable gargantuan dinner without which no Victorian

festivity was complete. After years of planning and preparation, Ipswich had its railway.

The Eastern Counties Railway Company had got its line from London as far as Colchester by 1843, when funds were exhausted. Ipswich businessmen could catch the 7 a.m. *Quicksilver* coach to Colchester, and get the train from there: this gave them five hours in London and still allowed them to return home that night. But there was a general feeling that, for a town like Ipswich, this was not good enough. A long poem appeared in an Ipswich newspaper, the last verse of which read:

> Men of Ipswich! – as ye value
> Worth of Mercantile renown,
> Be in bond of union acting,
> Claim a railway through your town.

The agitation was led by John Chevallier Cobbold, who first represented Ipswich in Parliament in 1847, and a group of prominent men of the time. They insisted that 'facilities for quick transit were of the utmost importance to an agricultural district and a commercial port'. An Act of Parliament allowed them to raise capital and form the Eastern Union Railway Company to build the line from Ipswich to Colchester.

The first Ipswich station was not intended to be permanent. When it opened, engineers were already at work, tunnelling through Stoke Hill, and a celebration dinner for the workmen was actually held in the tunnel in September 1846. When the new station was opened, in July 1860, it was on the town side of the hill, but there was none of the excitement of fourteen years earlier, for people had grown used to the railway. The only concession to the occasion was that 'some slight decorations of flowers and ribbons were hung upon the engines which, however, failed to lend gaiety and grace to the huge and unlithesome proportions which they were intended to adorn'. It was the end of the former peace of Stoke Hill where, previously, 'on a quiet Sunday evening . . . people could sit on the grass and distinguish the airs played by the military band at the Cavalry Barracks', right over on the far side of the town. Soon after this, new housing areas were carved out of the Stoke Hall Estate, and the two windmills which had stood on the hill since 1786 became dilapidated.

The 1840s and 1850s were years of the phenomenon sometimes known as 'Railway Mania'. In December 1846, a line was opened between Ipswich and Bury St Edmunds, the two Suffolk capitals. Twenty-seven miles (43·2 kilometres) were built in only sixteen months, with 2,000,000 cubic yards (approx. 1,500,000 metres³)

of earth moved, and more than a hundred bridges built, mostly by the manual labour of railway 'navvies'. A goods train, making a trial run with 70 tons (71·12 tonnes) of coal, before the official opening, promised well for the line's economic success when it reduced the price of coal in Bury by more than 10 per cent. The station buildings along this line are an interesting series. There was a strong feeling that, just because buildings were industrial or institutional, it did not follow that they should be ill-designed and spoil the natural beauty of the countryside in which they stood. These stations, the work of Frederick Barnes, an Ipswich architect, all have something of the look of country-houses, or at least lodges to country-houses. Those at Needham Market and Stowmarket are especially pleasing examples.

The Norwich to London route used to run via Cambridge. When, in 1849, it was diverted instead through Haughley, this provided a rail link between Ipswich and Norwich. When, ten years later, the East Suffolk line connected Ipswich to Lowestoft and Great Yarmouth, Suffolk's main railway system was complete. The second half of the century saw the construction of several smaller lines, bringing the towns and countryside closer together. There was the Mid-Suffolk Light Railway from Haughley to Laxfield, the Waveney Valley line, and the famous narrow-gauge line from Halesworth to Southwold, which operated from 1879 to 1929. A Late Victorian guide-book called it 'that quaintest of toy railways' and said that nobody took it

THE SOUTHWOLD EXPRESS - THE GUARD AS A PROFITABLE SIDELINE - PUTS THE DINNERS OF THE COTTAGERS ALONG THE ROUTE ON THE UP TRAIN - THESE BEING DONE TO PERFECTION BY THE RETURN JOURNEY - THE PROCESS OF CURING THE RENOWNED SOUTHWOLD BLOATERS IS SHEWN

A really cheap excursion

seriously except its own officials. 'If you happen to get left behind, it is possible to run after the train and catch it up at Walberswick.' Rhubarb and wild strawberries grew in profusion along sections of the line. Even now, a few derelict carriages can be found in that district, in use as garden-sheds and chicken-houses.

All the Suffolk railways were built to serve the freight needs of farming communities. Along their tracks travelled the raw materials for local industries: coal, fertilizers, and animal feeding-stuffs. Back came agricultural produce and the farming machinery made by firms like Ransomes of Ipswich and Garretts of Leiston.

People benefited from this new form of travel, too, though, even at its cheapest rates, rail travel was still very expensive for most of them. Excursions were occasionally offered at reduced rates. Only a few days after the opening celebrations, an excursion was run from Ipswich to Rotterdam – probably the first combined rail and sea trip to be arranged to the Continent by an East Anglian railway. Extra trains were laid on to take cricket enthusiasts to watch the M.C.C. at Bury in 1847, and to Mistley Regatta and to Framlingham Agricultural Show. There were frequent cheap day return trips to London, like the one in the advertisement illustrated on this page. And after Bank Holidays were introduced in 1871, seaside villages like Felixstowe, Aldeburgh, and

Southwold became popular and thriving towns, visited by more and more people. The Orwell estuary harbour development of Felixstowe was almost entirely the creation of Colonel Tomline, who brought the railway there in 1877, hoping to develop a port to rival Harwich. Lowestoft is perhaps the best example of what the railway could do for an existing small town by making it possible to get fish, while it was still fresh, quickly and cheaply to the big inland towns. The number of ships using Lowestoft rose from 410 in 1845 to 1,636 only six years later. At the same time, Lowestoft developed as a seaside resort. In 1874, it featured in Trollope's novel *The Way We Live Now*, and by the end of the century it was being described as 'one of the best and most agreeable watering-places on the East Coast'.

The 1840s, which saw the railway arrive, also saw the creation of the Wet-Dock at Ipswich, and the first real development of the port. Traffic on the Orwell in the early nineteenth century outstripped the facilities available. Commissioners had been appointed by Parliament, in 1805, to deepen, straighten, and generally improve the river, meeting the cost by levying duties on shipping and goods, but the Orwell was still left almost entirely dry at low water, and banks of shingle and silt were visible opposite the quays. Even so, trade was on the increase. The port duties were £30,000 in 1834 and £36,000 in 1836, when John Chevalier Cobbold began to lead the agitation for a wet-dock. An eminent engineer's report suggested making a new channel (the 'New Cut') for the River Orwell,

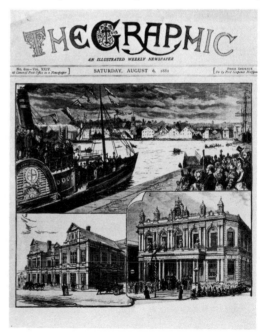

damming the river's old course, and shutting it off by lock gates to form an enclosed basin of some 33 acres (13 hectares). The plan was adopted and a special Act of Parliament obtained, one of the first to be signed by Queen Victoria only ten days after her accession, in 1837. The work took five years, and was the subject of much ill-feeling in the town, some of whose inhabitants (and the local Press) thought it unnecessary. The eventual cost was more than twice the original estimate. But when the lock gates closed for the first time in January 1842, Ipswich found herself in possession of the largest dock on the east coast between London and Hull. Within a year the navigation dues had doubled their annual average, and they doubled again in another decade.

Along with its new dock, in 1843 Ipswich rebuilt the Old Custom House, the first of the series of fine buildings the town still has, and uses, from the Victorian Age. The handsome building, with its portico and double external staircase, still presides over the dock, even though now dwarfed by the granaries and warehouses all round it. Eighty orphans from the local workhouse came to see the opening ceremony. They carried a banner which bore the words: 'Though Poor, Happy and Grateful.'

The first Museum, in the street of that name, opened in 1847. When the Prince Consort came to lay the foundation-stone of Ipswich School, a few years later he spent some hours at the Museum. The Queen reported that he talked of little else for days. The 1860s saw important changes in the town centre, on the Cornhill. The old Town Hall, with some adjoining properties, were cleared away, and the present dignified building erected. A week of celebrations marked its opening in January 1868, and a local music-teacher wrote the 'New Town Hall Polka' specially for the occasion. Within a few more years, the Post Office went up beside the Town Hall, and the Corn Exchange (now an Entertainments Centre) behind it. A new Museum, in High Street, replaced the original little building, already too small. Post Office and Museum were opened on the same day – 27 July 1881 – along with new lock gates to increase the efficiency of the dock. The illustration on page 56 shows these three new amenities celebrated together on the front page of a leading weekly newspaper.

Ipswich Custom House, designed by J. M. Clarke, 1843

The Suffolk Show, Christchurch Park, Ipswich, 1869. The artist, John Duvall, is the seated figure in the foreground.

CHAPTER 16
AGRICULTURE

In the nineteenth century, railways contributed to the expansion of Suffolk's two main towns, Ipswich and Lowestoft, promoting the urbanization of the county in line with the rest of industrial Britain. But whereas in Britain as a whole, 80 per cent of the people now live in towns or suburbs, in Suffolk, in 1971, only 120,000 lived in Ipswich, and no more than 50,000 in Lowestoft, out of the county total of some 550,000. The great shift in the balance, with Britain changing from a predominantly rural to a predominantly urban community in the mid nineteenth century, did not happen in Suffolk. Nevertheless, while the towns and villages both tended to increase in population down to the middle of the century, after that time it was a different story. Ipswich and Lowestoft went on increasing steadily, while the rural parishes reached their peak, then started a descent, at least in the size of their population, as people from the villages went to work in the towns.

The Industrial Revolution, which improved transport and led to factory production in the towns, affected the countryside's great industry – farming – in precisely the opposite way. With each new improvement made by the farm-implement manufacturers of Ipswich and Bury, Leiston and Peasenhall, the old Suffolk world of the Suffolk Punch and the Lord of the Harvest, the straight single horse-drawn furrow, and harvesting by scythe and sickle, took a step backwards into the past.

And this is to say nothing of the series of 'depressions' which affected Suffolk farming at intervals all through the period dividing the Napoleonic Wars from the Second World War, and which took their toll, as readers of Ronald Blythe's *Akenfield*, and the books of George Ewart Evans, will know.

FARMING IN THE NINETEENTH CENTURY
The nineteenth century saw alternate periods of depression and prosperity for farmers. High grain prices during the wars with Napoleon encouraged many of them to change from dairy to arable farming. In 1846, when the Corn Laws were repealed, cheap corn could be imported, so British farmers suffered. Things improved in 1854, when the Crimean War stimulated demand for another ten years or so: the heavy lands especially shared the all-round prosperity then. Manufacturers of

farm implements co-operated, so that farmers got what they most needed and what best served their land. By mid century the region was being quoted by agricultural writers as a splendid example of estate management.

This 'Golden Age' came to an end about 1870, and from then until the end of the century, Suffolk was one of the most depressed counties of England. A continuous series of bad harvests combined with cheap imported foreign produce to defeat the farmers. In 1879, the 'Black Year', the summer was wet almost from start to finish: the harvest was still being gathered in October, and by mid November severe winter weather had set in. Landlords reduced their rents. Farms that became vacant were let 'at any rates that can be obtained' in the ensuing years. One estate which had cost £4,000 in 1874 fetched only £900 when it was sold in 1897. In that same year, land was being sold at £16 an acre that had cost three times as much in 1870. Much of the lighter heathland went out of cultivation altogether and reverted to rabbit-warrens or game-bird reserves. (When the Forestry Commission began tree-planting in the early 1920s in West Suffolk, they first had to kill 83,000 rabbits.) Farmers on the heavy lands economized on labour, used less manure, kept fewer stock, and allowed some of their land to go to grass. Some landlords sold up completely, or let their land to shooting tenants. The whole community suffered, but farm labourers suffered most. They were usually, even then, still employed on a daily, or hourly, basis, which made it easy for farmers to put them on short time, or lay them off in bad weather and so save money like that. Harvest piecework was their only chance to earn any kind of bonus. Wages in Suffolk tended to lag behind those elsewhere: labourers at Exning, near Newmarket, were agitating in 1874 for a rise from 13s to 14s (65p to 70p) a week, while their Lincolnshire counterparts were getting 18s (90p). By 1893, after years of depression, the average Suffolk farmworker was only earning 12s (60p) a week.

THE BEGINNING OF CO-OPERATIVE SCHEMES

The bad years tested the farmers' initiative and ingenuity. Poultry-keeping increased, and more satisfactory and profitable ways were found of marketing eggs. In 1903 a local scheme began in the Framlingham area, and subsequently expanded, whereby farmers sold their eggs to a central collecting organization: this was the start of the co-operative movement in farming, now much more extensive. The year 1904 saw the formation of the group called 'Eastern Counties Farmers', now operating in eight counties, of which Suffolk is one. It sells its farmer members various requisites, such as machinery, seed, and animal feeding-stuffs, and it buys and markets their own produce for them, as well as providing expert advice when they need it.

FARMING SINCE 1914

In the First World War, when we needed to produce as much of our own food as possible, Government subsidies and guaranteed prices gave a boost to farming. But when this encouragement was withdrawn, depression set in again: between 1920 and 1922 the price of wheat almost halved, and wages fell from 46s to 30s (£2.30 to £1.50) per week. Some farmers went bankrupt, others had to leave land uncultivated because they could not afford to buy seed corn for sowing.

The last thirty to forty years have probably seen more change in the Suffolk countryside than any previous period. The Second World War once more made home production of foodstuffs essential.

Harvesting by hand: a scything team at Wenham in 1888

59

Farmers were given financial help to drain and clean neglected land. Prices for crops were fixed which made it profitable to grow them once more. Scientific methods – for example, mineral fertilizers and chemical weed-killers – which were increasingly used during the war, continued to be used when it was over. As a result of all the changes, farming remains the basic industry of Suffolk, and prospers within the limits set by Government policies and the contrariness of the weather. But the old village communities have changed almost out of recognition.

MANUFACTURERS OF AGRICULTURAL MACHINERY
A book published in 1850, *The Dictionary of the Farm*, said there was no part of England where the implements of husbandry were more perfect than in Suffolk, or where new crops were tried with more readiness and less prejudice.

Ransomes of Ipswich. The large firm of Ransomes, Sims & Jefferies began in 1789 when a Norfolk man, Robert Ransome, started a business in Old Foundry Road in Ipswich, making cast-iron ploughshares and appointing agents throughout Norfolk and Suffolk to market them. In 1803, he made the accidental discovery of how to 'chill' these shares, to make them harder and more effective, and then patented a plough body that could be dismantled, for repairs to be carried out in the fields.

The Royal Agricultural Society's first show in 1839 gave Ransomes a gold medal for their implements and machinery, which now included lawn-mowers. They won three medals at the Great Exhibition of 1851 and four first prizes for their ploughs at the Newcastle Royal Show of 1864. Queen Victoria bought one of their lawn-mowers: her son, Edward VII, saw a motorized one demonstrated on the lawns of Buckingham Palace in 1904. The following year, W. G. Grace wrote to the firm: 'Your motor lawn mowers, used on the London County Council cricket ground last season, did very well.'

The First World War turned Ransomes to making munitions, with some 5,000 employees. One of their first aeroplanes brought down a Zeppelin airship at Theberton, near Leiston. There were lean years after the war, when they concentrated on developing large-scale grass-cutters for parks and golf-courses, as well as on consolidating their overseas connections in Africa, India, Australia, and the Americas. The year 1939 brought more war work, including the development of a small tractor for use on market gardens and smallholdings, helping the drive to produce as much food as possible at home. Since the war, the factories have turned out an enormous range of mainly agricultural machinery, such as grain-driers, tractors, and combine-harvesters, as well as grass-cutters of all kinds and sizes.

Garretts of Leiston. Richard Garrett, founder of the firm, was born in 1757 at Woodbridge. When he married, he set up in business at Leiston as a sickle-maker. His son, Richard II, married the daughter of a Norfolk man, Balls, who designed the first effective threshing-machine. Balls and Garrett began building these machines, and their business expanded. When Richard III took over in 1836, there were sixty employees. In the next two decades this number increased to 600, and the site of the works covered 7 acres (2·8 hectares). Garretts' machinery was known all over Europe.

The firm specialized in adapting its tools to the farmers' needs. Threshing-machines remained their most important line – eight were entered at the Cambridge Royal Show in 1840 – but they also made drills, horse-hoes, chaff-cutters, ploughs, barley-hummellers (for removing barley awns), winnowers, dressers, and hay-making machinery. In the 1850s they earned 110 awards from agricultural societies, and took gold medals at London, Paris, and Vienna. By 1861 their catalogues were being printed

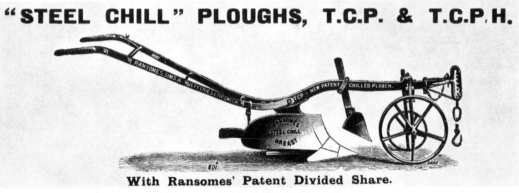

"STEEL CHILL" PLOUGHS, T.C.P. & T.C.P.H.

With Ransomes' Patent Divided Share.

A Ransome plough, from an early catalogue

in four languages, and they employed agents in India, Australia, North America, Africa, and Europe.

In the years of the Depression, almost all the firm's output went overseas. From the turn of the century they concentrated on developing steam-power, and its application to both farming and road transport. Garretts were taken over, in 1932, by Beyer Peacock, a Manchester company, and produced munitions in the Second World War. In the 1960s, the old works were demolished and moved to a site near by where, with more than 400 employees, they continue to make machine tools and dry-cleaning equipment, and run an iron-foundry. They also have a training department for about thirty engineering apprentices. All this operates now under the name 'Richard Garrett Engineering Ltd'.

James Smyth of Peasenhall. In the closing years of the eighteenth century, James Smyth and his brother set up in business at Peasenhall, near Framlingham, as wheelwrights repairing seed-drills. They developed their own Smyth drill, whose coulters could be raised or lowered for different kinds of work. Expansion was slow, but by the end of last century the firm was employing a hundred men. A good deal of their business came from abroad. The last member of the family involved in the company died in 1908, and operations (by that time under a different name) ceased altogether in 1967.

FERTILIZERS

The value of Crag (see Chapter 1) as a fertilizer, and to correct acidity in the soil, was recognized but not exploited in the eighteenth century. In the 1840s, J. S. Henslow, Professor of Botany and Mineralogy at Cambridge University, Rector of Hitcham, and President of Ipswich Museum, realized that the coprolites in the Red Crag had a phosphate value. In 1843, Edward Packard of Snape began to grind them in an old flour-mill, and decompose them in sulphuric acid: then a few years later he began manufacturing superphosphates at premises in Ipswich and Bramford. The peninsula between the Orwell and Deben rivers is rich in coprolites and many pits were dug there. By 1877, 10,000 tons (10,161 tonnes) were being sold each year: barges brought cattle-food and manure to the riverside quays, and left loaded with coprolites. As much as £20 worth could sometimes be dug from cottage gardens at Waldringfield. After 1893, phosphatic material was being made more cheaply in other ways, and the pits were no longer worked.

Packard's firm united, in 1929, with two similar local ones, to form Fison, Packard & Prentice Ltd. The new company went on to acquire thirty-two other fertilizer companies throughout Britain, and

An Ipswich street-name recalls a nineteenth-century industry

in 1942 they adopted the simpler name of Fisons Ltd. One of their several large factories is at Ipswich, and they also have a research establish-ment at Levington and offices at Felixstowe. The products of Fisons Ltd are internationally known and used, and extend well beyond their original range of agricultural supplies.

THE SUGAR-BEET INDUSTRY

Suffolk farming has changed more through the introduction of sugar-beet than anything else. It has been called the 'solid lifebelt to which the drowning farmer could cling'.

Like most innovations, it was regarded with mistrust at first. An early attempt to set up a sugar-factory in Lavenham in 1868 failed, partly through suspicion of this new crop, partly from the lack of finance and the limitations of the primitive equipment available. It took the 1925 Beet Sugar Subsidy Act to stimulate and revive the industry. The Ipswich and Bury sugar-factories were both built that year. A crisis came in 1934 when it seemed for a time that Government support might be withdrawn, but the importance of continuing sugar production at home was, happily, recognized and the factories survived. Farmers quickly found that contracting to grow beet for a guaranteed price paid them better than growing turnips or swedes to feed to sheep. There was a cash return for the sugar extracted, and a further bonus, because each acre of beet produces, as well as 2 tons (2 tonnes) of sugar, another 2 tons (2 tonnes) of leaves and crowns, and more than 1 ton (1 tonne) of pulp, all useful for cattle-feed.

Greater understanding of fertilizers, the increas-ing use of machinery, and the application of science, have all helped boost the crop. Barrow, in the west of Suffolk, has a research station where beet culture is examined and tested. Little was done before the Second World War towards mechanization. William Catchpole of Stanton designed a beet-harvester in 1937: it was built by Robert Boby Ltd of Bury, and several were sold locally. After the war, in 1946, a demonstration of all makes of harvesters was held, and Catchpole's created great interest. Drills, ploughs, mechanical cleaners, and other labour-saving equipment have all been introduced and regularly improved so that a high degree of mechanization has been achieved in the beet industry. The factories begin processing in the autumn and continue right through the winter. They operate a system of permits to control their intake: this avoids the possibility of more loads arriving than can be dealt with at one time.

Progress in the sugar-beet industry in its first ten years

	No. of growers	No. of acres (hectares) grown
1925	901	4,626 (1,870)
1930	1,680	14,907 (6,030)
1935	2,024	21,016 (8,510)

Increased mechanization in the sugar-beet industry in Suffolk

	Amount of total crop harvested mechanically (%)
1947	1
1950	16
1953	30
1963	75

MECHANIZATION IN FARMING

Steam-power. Garretts were taking prizes at Royal Agricultural Society shows as early as 1849 for their portable steam-engine, for threshing and other agricultural purposes. Steam-ploughs, with the plough moving across the field on a belt driven by twin steam-engines, one either side, did useful work in breaking up the heavy soils when more land was being brought into cultivation in both world wars. But in general, steam tackle went out of use after the 1920s. It was last used, in the Hadleigh area, in 1945.

Tractors. Fordson tractors from the U.S.A. were imported in 1914 and used on Suffolk farms. By the 1930s, most farms of more than 150 acres (61 hectares) had a tractor. After 1949, British-made Ferguson tractors and trailers began to replace horses and tumbrils, especially in the sugar-beet fields. Their hydraulic operation made them easy to handle. Tractors are used in ploughing, drilling, beet-harvesting, spring cultivating, and general transport work. Their use has made possible deeper ploughing, from 8 to 12 in (20 to 30 cm) instead of 5 to 6 in (13 to 15 cm) as before. This has made a great difference to the lighter lands of the county.

Harvesting machinery. The combine-harvester is the most revolutionary piece of equipment to be introduced on the farm. In 1942 there were thirty-two in Suffolk. By 1968 that number had risen to 2,970, an average of six to each parish. With the combine, getting in the harvest, which a century ago was a two- to three-week job for a team of reapers, can be done by two men, and with less heed of the weather. Large fields are needed for the combine to operate efficiently and economically, so in some districts there is a tendency for farmers to uproot hedges and amalgamate a number of fields. Disposal of the straw after combining is sometimes difficult. In the 1960s it used to be burnt in the fields, but this practice is being discouraged by stricter controls. Methods are being found, lately, of gathering the straw in bales and removing it, for animal feed or litter.

Transport. Lorries used to come to the fields to collect produce in sacks. Now, more and more load directly from the harvesting operation. Peas and beans for canning-factories, or the Lowestoft freezing factory, leave the fields where they grew, in lorries. So does the sugar-beet bound for the Ipswich and Bury factories.

Crop-spraying. The use of chemical sprays to control weeds in crops began to be understood and appreciated in the 1950s. Between 1950 and 1956 the number of crop-spraying machines increased by 1,526. Herbicides to use in them are becoming increasingly selective and, therefore, more successful in use. More and more crops are sprayed from the air to check aphids, especially on sugar-beet and brassicas.

LIVESTOCK ON THE FARM

Horses. The horse is on the decline as a work animal. In 1939 there were 26,308; in 1975, 2,113. The chestnut horse called the 'Suffolk Punch' was

Suffolk Punch at Hollesley

perfected by Thomas Crisp, of Rendlesham and Gedgrave, in 1768. Five years later, he advertised it 'to get good stock for coach or road'. Samuel Pepys, in 1669, had heard the parents of fat children with short legs address them as Punches, and the name seems to have been applied to the horse because of those same characteristics. Its large stomach was an asset: horses began work at 6.30 a.m. and worked until 2.30 p.m. and, therefore, needed a substantial breakfast.

The Suffolk Stud Book describes the Punch as being 16 hands high, with a big head, and graceful in outline. It had a smart walk and a well-balanced trot. The long straight legs and big knees were free of hair, an advantage when the horse was working on clay land. It had splendid pulling power, well demonstrated in the First World War when Punches were used to haul heavy guns from mud-filled pits on the battlefields. Lord Clark, whose father owned the famous pedigree stud at Sudbourne Hall until 1918, wrote: 'I think that Suffolk Punches provided my earliest experience of sculptural beauty. The memory of their full, compact shapes and silky brown surfaces may still underlie my artistic judgments.'

Punches took the first prize for the best horse for agricultural purposes fourteen times in the first twenty-three of the the Royal Agricultural Society's shows. The 1960 Stud Book expressed regret that 'the breed should have diminished in numbers during the past few years'. A few studs remain, including one at H.M. Hollesley Bay Colony, near Woodbridge. In the early 1970s, twenty-four stallions and fifty-five mares were registered as belonging to Suffolk farmers. Punches remain among the most popular entries at the Suffolk Show every June.

Cattle. Black and white Friesians are the most numerous dairy cattle. The Red Poll breed, much less popular now, derived from the original Norfolk and Suffolk cattle, and was crossed in the 1960s with Danish Red cattle to improve the milk yield.

Dairy-farming has undergone great changes since the 1950s. Cows are often kept in a covered yard, with automatic dispensers for food and water, and the dung mechanically removed to storage-pits. The old-style cow-house is being replaced by the milking 'parlour' where one man can milk fifty or so cows. All these improvements mean that larger herds can be kept. Milk goes straight to stainless-steel tanks for collection by the Milk Marketing Board: another example of the collective system of marketing. Progress has been made in controlling disease. TB has been practically eradicated, and a free vaccination scheme keeps down brucellosis. Foot and mouth disease no longer presents a serious problem.

Sheep. When the price of corn fell, the number of sheep increased. When higher prices, or wartime needs, made arable farming profitable again, the number of sheep decreased. This 'up sheep and down corn' has been the general pattern in Suffolk, at least for the last hundred years.

The Suffolk breed was founded by crossing improved Southdown rams with Norfolk horned ewes. The name 'Suffolks' dates from 1859. The Suffolk Sheep Society, formed in 1886 to try and continue improvements through selective breeding, keeps records and has branches in Australia, New Zealand, Tasmania, Canada, South Africa, and the U.S.A. The Suffolk's best qualities are a high percentage of lean meat, and a short white dense fleece, yielding 8–10 lb (3–5 kg) of washed wool per animal. Other breeds found in Suffolk are the Southdown, Dorset Horn, and Dorset Down.

The introduction of sugar-beet farming in 1925 has had the most effect on sheep-farming. The beet replaced other root crops on which sheep once fed. So farm policy began to change, and the change was accelerated by the Second World War, when more grassland was ploughed up for arable.

Sheep are kept mainly on grass and brought in to the fold for winter. Lambing starts in January–February. At least one farmer has installed closed-circuit television in his fold, for the shepherd to be able to watch his ewes without disturbing them.

No. of sheep in Suffolk.

1959	95,203
1962	89,853
1968	61,363
1975	54,557

Pigs. There has been a steady increase since the Second World War, from 58,612 in 1944 to 536,445 in 1975. The majority of breeding sows are the Large White variety, with the Landrace standing next. Increasing attention to farrowing hygiene is reducing the number of piglets that once died of pneumonia. Stricter control of diet, the use of vaccines, and a policy of slaughtering where necessary, help reduce the incidence of swine fever. Suffolk has a number of bacon-factories which have encouraged improvements in pig-breeding, to obtain more length and a better proportion of lean to fat.

Poultry. Suffolk has shared the enormous boom in poultry-keeping since the end of the Second World War. In 1930, just under 500,000 were kept. The 1975 figure is more than 5,500,000. One hatchery alone, that at Barrow, produces more than 500,000 day-old chicks each year.

In 1950–55, much consideration was given to how to increase egg production by better housing. The introduction of the deep-litter system (where birds are kept in sheds on a layer of straw), and the provision of extra hours of artificial light, both helped. Battery cages (in fact first used in Suffolk in 1938, at Occold) were brought into use. The larger numbers of birds that could be kept under these conditions made poultry-keeping profitable and not just a sideline for the farmer's wife. By 1968 Suffolk stood fourth in England and Wales for the production of broiler fowls. Some farms have their own packing-stations, where the birds are processed and packed, and sometimes frozen, for sale. Chickens remain the most popular. In 1975 there were only 321,868 turkeys and 84,301 ducks and geese.

There were enormous losses from fowl pest in the 1950s. Improvement has come about with the use of vaccines and, where considered necessary, restrictions on the movement of all poultry.

Farming in Suffolk: 1975

(a) *Crops*

	Acres grown	%
Barley	254,897	42·20
Wheat	155,673	25·78
Sugar-beet	60,129	9·96
Vegetables	33,837	5·60
Crops for stock-feed (beans, turnips, kale, mangolds, cabbage, etc.)	21,427	3.55
Woodland	16,098	2·67
Fallow	13,904	2·30
Oats	11,868	1·97
Potatoes	9,545	1·58
Orchards and fruit	7,097	1·18
Maize	6,167	1·02
Rye	5,938	0·98
Lucerne	5,732	0·95
Soft fruit	1,305	0·22
Bulbs and flowers	272	0·04
Total	603,889	100

(b) *Livestock*

	Number kept	%
All poultry	5,690,414	89·99
Pigs	536,445	8·48
Sheep and lambs	54,557	0·86
Dairy cattle	27,149	0·43
Beef cattle	11,686	0·19
Horses	2,113	
Bulls	783	0·05
Goats	231	
Total	6,323,378	100

(c) *Labour*

Full-time workers	6,662 males	Total
	455 females	7,117
Part-time workers	826 males	Total
	1,462 females	2,288

Total number employed in agriculture, as full- or part-time workers, seasonal workers, farmers, managers, directors, partners, etc. 16,372

Ploughing in the mid 1970s

Workmen from Ransome & Rapier's on an outing to Dedham, early this century

CHAPTER 17
THE ECONOMY OF SUFFOLK

In the Middle Ages, East Anglia was a major industrial region. It declined in the seventeenth century, and then the Industrial Revolution drew the remnants of cloth-making away to the steeper mill-streams and coal areas of the Midlands and North Country. The coming of the railway in the nineteenth century speeded up the process of dispersal. Fortunately, in the later nineteenth century, Suffolk benefited from the increasing tendency of certain industries to move out of London, a move which has gone on into our own day. A printing firm set itself up in Beccles in 1873, for example, and by 1900 silk-weaving was well established in the old Stour Valley weaving district, especially at Sudbury, which became the headquarters of the Spitalfields silk firms. Most towns whose transport facilities were reasonably good had maltings. Rapid agricultural developments both at home and overseas were reflected in the growth of the large engineering works described in Chapter 16. In agriculture's depressed years, when local markets could absorb less, such industries adapted their products, so that instead of catering mainly for local needs, they were soon exporting their goods all over the world.

This growth of manufacturing since 1870 has brought certain benefits. It has provided employment for people who would otherwise have moved out of the county. Small country towns, whose functions as markets and social centres were declining, have been partly compensated by the new industries established in them. The range of amenities has consequently improved, and a higher standard of living has been made possible.

FROM 1900 TO 1939

The depressed state of agriculture at the close of the nineteenth century reduced incomes and led to unemployment. This inevitably encouraged numbers of people to emigrate from Suffolk altogether, and, by reducing the wages of those who remained, it reduced considerably the demand for the products of local industries. Brewers and shoe-makers, to take two very different local producers, found that their sales decreased when people had to make less money stretch further.

As transport facilities improved, country-dwellers were brought into closer touch with the big towns than they had been previously, and began to go there for most of their shopping. So the larger villages and smaller towns found their functions gradually usurped. Hadleigh, in White's *Directory* of 1885, had ten shoemakers, ten dressmakers and milliners, and seven outfitters listed among its inhabitants. In the 1929 *Directory* the figures for those same trades were only five, four, and four, respectively.

The First World War caused a number of firms to switch to small-scale engineering, or some form of wartime production. Afterwards, when the demand for munitions and wartime equipment had passed, some of the smaller of these firms found difficulty in returning to the old peacetime ways. Those who could not afford to change their pattern of production by investing in up-to-date machinery often failed to survive the hazards of peace, and the general depression of the 1920s and 1930s.

Where new industries did spread into country towns, development was helped by the increasing availability of electricity as a source of power. Silk-weaving, and corset and clothing manufacture, were brought to Sudbury and Hadleigh, light engineer-ing to Framlingham, bacon-curing to Elmswell, saw-milling and woodworking to Brandon, Beccles, and Bures. And the introduction of sugar-beet, already the salvation of many hard-pressed farmers, created employment for large numbers at the two sugar-factories of Ipswich and Bury.

AFTER 1939

The Second World War did not, on the whole, change the pattern of industry in Suffolk greatly. In 1946, engineering, food and drink production, and brush and coconut-matting manufacture still employed two out of every three workers. One thing the war did was to create a shortage of labour, and, partly because of this, wages almost doubled their pre-war average, hours of work were reduced, and a greater prosperity was spread over a wider area. With labour at a premium, those who had once had little alternative to domestic work, or casual work in agriculture, found that their skills – or the lack of them – were in demand in the towns, in those industries which were struggling to get back to a peacetime footing. A number of trades, such as clothing manufacture, which had always been able to recruit most of their employees directly from schools, began to find competition from some of the newer industries, which offered juveniles more attractive working conditions. The raising of the school-leaving age in 1944 further aggravated the situation.

OVERSPILL AND EXPANSION

One of the most far-reaching decisions for Suffolk was that made by the West Suffolk County Council (when the two halves still operated independently) to increase their population dramatically by 1981, by inviting the London County Council to re-site factories and their employees in West Suffolk, on a large scale. As a result of this agreement, Sudbury, Hadleigh, Haverhill, Mildenhall, Brandon, and Bury St Edmunds developed industrial estates on their fringes, accompanied by large and mostly unattractive housing estates near by. While this had the effect of increasing the population, and providing new and welcome sources of employ-ment, it also, partly at least, helped to destroy small and once-agreeable towns, through the con-struction in and round them of the inevitable new roads and impersonal shopping centres, and acres of ill-conceived housing sprawling out across the landscape. It is questionable whether Haverhill, for instance, can be a town in any truly urban sense: it seems likely to remain a suburban community without the central amenities that provide some justification for suburbs. Only Bury seems to have a good chance of developing in an intelligible urban and civilized way, but even here a whole section of housing and industry is being developed on the far side of the new by-pass. The lessons of the admirable English post-war New Towns have been almost completely ignored in Suffolk. A promising development was planned in the late 1960s for Ipswich, but was suppressed by the Government for lack of funds.

Ipswich, now (1975) a town of 122,000 inhabitants, has always been the focus of business and social activity for a wide area. Its position at the lowest possible crossing-place of the River Orwell ensured that any road from the south to the east of East Anglia had to go through it. Indeed, its main thoroughfare – Westgate Street, Tavern Street, Carr Street – is probably on the line of the prehistoric coastal trackway skirting the edge of the primitive forest. The nineteenth century was a period of steady expansion, accelerated after the 1840s brought the railway and built the wet-dock (see Chapter 15). Old industries grew, and new ones were founded. Some were traditional, based on the town's agricultural background; some were new. In recent years the growth of the port of Ipswich has made it one of the leading ports for trade to and from Europe.

(Opposite) Lowestoft: Workers on a salvage tug watch a sister ship being launched at Brooke Marine.

Ransomes, Sims and Jefferies, with their associate firms of Ransomes and Marles, and Ransome and Rapier, employ several thousands of people, producing industrial trucks and cranes, and hydraulically operated excavators, as well as the world-famous powered lawn-mowers (see Chapter 16). Crane Limited, founded in 1921, employ over 2,000 on their 42 acre (17 hectare) site. Their valves and heating boilers are exported all over the world. Bull Motors, and Cocksedge and Company are among the other large engineering firms, and the firm of Delta, making brass, manganese, and aluminium bronze, is part of Europe's biggest brass-manufacturing group. The quayside has large malthouses and flour-mills, Fisons' fertilizer plant, and the Cliff Brewery, where Tollemache and Cobbold's latest plant can fill 1,500 dozen bottles of beer in an hour. The latter's transport fleet of more than a hundred vehicles supplies the 380-or-so Tolly-Cobbold public houses and over 50 off-licensed premises throughout Suffolk. At Cliff Quay, the vast post-war generating-station, with its three chimneys 325 feet (100 metres) high, the first thing you see when arriving from London by rail, supplies the town and a wide surrounding area with electricity. Other industries include boat-building, steel-piling manufacture, tobacco and cigarettes, printing, ready-to-wear sports clothing, sacks and bags, and marquees for large functions.

Ipswich has its own fleet of motor-buses for public transport. There are indoor and outdoor swimming-baths, and more than 500 acres (202 hectares) of parks and playing-fields. Christchurch Park, close to the town centre, has one of Ipswich's two museums, housed in a Tudor mansion of 1548. The Victorian Corn Exchange has, in 1975, been converted and adapted as an admirable entertainment centre. The Civic College, opened in 1961, provides, as well as its regular courses, part-time further education for large numbers of students,

sent there by the firms they work for, on the day-release system. Evening classes attract students from outside the town as well as those who live there.

Since the war, many old housing areas have been demolished, and widespreading new estates built on the town's outskirts. Development in Ipswich itself has been less careful, but a welcome recent innovation is an experimental scheme to reduce and almost eliminate motor traffic from the main shopping streets in the centre.

Lowestoft, Suffolk's second largest town (53,260 in 1975), was an important fishing-port even in the fourteenth century, but owes its modern position largely to Samuel Morton Peto, the 'maker of Lowestoft', who began to create a major port there in 1844. The railway's arrival made it possible to get the Dogger Bank catches to Billingsgate without delay. Lowestoft's population rose by 50 per cent in the next decade, and has gone on rising. In the early 1970s it was reckoned that 15 per cent of the inhabitants of Lowestoft were, in some way, employed in fishing and its associated industries.

The British Transport Dock Undertaking is planning to rebuild the Victorian docks to make Lowestoft one of the most up-to-date and efficient ports in the country. It already stands next to Grimsby, Hull, and Fleetwood in importance for fishing. More than seventy deep-sea trawlers operate from Lowestoft, making ten-day trips, some 300 miles (420 kilometres) out into the north-east sector of the North Sea. Eighty per cent of the catch is plaice and cod, the rest is made up mainly of turbot, sole, and haddock. Half goes straight to factories at the quayside, to be frozen and packed for shops and supermarkets. In 1920, the Ministry of Agriculture and Fisheries set up an establishment here, to carry out research and international sea-fishery investigations; ideas and methods have all changed a great deal in recent years. Other boats are engaged in servicing the numerous gas and oil installations in the North Sea. The Brooke Marine shipyards build and repair trawlers, and the firm of Eastern Coachworks builds bodies for a number of leading motor-bus operators.

In its other capacity, Lowestoft is a flourishing seaside resort, with two piers, parks, gardens, and hotels. Its position on the east coast makes it a favourite holiday centre for visitors from the Midlands, who can get there easily. Lake Lothing connects Lowestoft with Oulton Broad, a gateway to 200 miles (320 kilometres) of attractive inland waterways, whose 'season' extends almost throughout the year. Catering for holiday-makers, directly or indirectly, is one of the most important sources of employment for the people of Lowestoft itself and the adjoining settlements of Pakefield and Kessingland.

Bury St Edmunds. On one of his 'Rural Rides', in 1830, William Cobbett was asked (by the people of Ipswich!) whether he did not think Bury 'the nicest town in the world'. It expanded steadily in the nineteenth century, especially after the coming of the railway in 1846, and by 1878 had spread out to the west as far as the Gibraltar Barracks, home of the Suffolk Regiment before it was absorbed into the Royal Anglian Regiment. Redoubled expansion since the end of the Second World War has increased the resident population to 26,800 (1975), while another 70,000 come to Bury for work, shopping, and recreation. The Theatre Royal was rescued in the 1960s from being a barrel-store for the local brewery, and now provides a home for both professional and local dramatic productions.

The Western Trading Estate was begun in 1955, and its 30 acre (12 hectare) site has attracted national and international firms. After the Council's decision to receive London overspill, an Eastern Trading Estate was started. The first firm to set up there was Associated British Maltsters, and many of the subsequent settlers have been connected with agriculture.

The sugar-beet factory which was established in 1925 is England's largest, and handles in an average year 800,000 tons (800,000 tonnes) of beet, from which it extracts 100,000 tons (100,000 tonnes) of sugar. Some 270 people work there permanently.

Market-day at Bury St Edmunds

Brewing (Greene King Limited) is another traditional industry. The Howard Rotovator Company won a Queen's Award for Industry in April 1976. Apart from these, some of the principal manufactures are clothing, animal foods, roadmaking equipment, miniature filament lamps, photographic and TV equipment, steel furniture, sugar confectionery, and colourings and flavourings for the bakery trade. Training in subjects associated with these and other industries is available at the College of Further Education. Bury's new hospital is one of the best in East Anglia, embodying the latest ideas of treatment and accommodation.

Felixstowe with a population of 19,460 in 1975 was a quiet seaside village in the nineteenth century. It developed its present dual character as seaside town and seaport after the arrival of the railway in 1877, and the 1875 Act of Parliament which set up the Felixstowe Dock and Railway Company. The railway helped the town grow into a popular resort, with a 2 mile (3·2 kilometre) promenade (1902). The docks, officially opened in 1887, were used by twenty-eight foreign ships in 1904. By 1914 Felixstowe was known for its excellent moorings: it became a naval base for destroyers and minesweepers, and the R.A.F. had a flying-boat base there. Commercial progress was slowed down by the war and its aftermath. The Second World War saw an Air Sea Rescue base established in the dock basin, and ammunition stored in the warehouses. By 1951, when the port was thoroughly run down, a new management team began to renovate the old buildings and cranes, and revive the foreign trade. New roads and rail-tracks were made, and warehouses built, so that the docks now represent a multi-million pound investment.

A fundamentally important step was taken in 1966 with the inauguration of a container terminal on a 2,040 foot (628 metre) quay. At the factories manufactured goods can be crated directly into vast boxes, or containers, and brought to the port by road or rail: no further loading or unloading is necessary, so the risk of damage is minimal. There are special handling machines, and 60 acres (24 hectares) of land is available for waiting containers. Cargo for western Europe, Scandinavia, the Far East, Australasia, and the U.S.A. is all shipped this way.

A terminal to handle the export of cars was opened in 1973. The next year, the largest single shipment of cars ever to leave England went via Felixstowe to the U.S.A. There are four roll-on/roll-off terminals to create a link with Europe. Modern methods, with cranes and fork-lift trucks, have speeded the export process. Much cargo bound eventually for the Middle East goes from Felixstowe in this way. There are vast cold stores,

and plenty of bulk tank storage for liquids such as fuel and chemicals.

The Company plans to encourage passenger traffic to Europe through Felixstowe as an alternative to the south coast ports. European Ferries began operating thrice-daily sailings to Zeebrugge in the summer of 1975.

To cope with the enormously increased volume of traffic, the A45 road between Ipswich and Felixstowe has been improved, and a spur road taken off so that dock-bound traffic no longer needs to go near the town. At its opposite end, Felixstowe continues to develop steadily as a popular seaside and holiday resort.

CONTAINERS HANDLED AT FELIXSTOWE SINCE THE
SERVICE BEGAN

1967	18,522
1968	33,790
1969	74,033
1970	93,099
1971	89,518
1972	106,336
1973	134,103
1974	137,850

Other towns. In the west (the County of West Suffolk until 1974), Haverhill (12,421), Sudbury (8,860), and Hadleigh (5,420), formerly small market-towns, have all grown under the London overspill scheme. Haverhill has replaced its old textile industry by others ranging from general engineering to the sophisticated electronic and telecommunications equipment of Pye Limited. Others include a butter-packing plant, a large Co-operative Wholesale Society bakery, and the manufacture of brushes, ropes, and sacking. Sudbury has created an industrial estate, with manufacturers of agricultural machinery and hydraulic equipment. Here, expansion has extended to the neighbouring village of Great Cornard, whose population has swollen to almost 7,000. Like the others, Hadleigh has its industrial estate with new industries, but retains also its important livestock market, serving a wide surrounding area.

In the Breckland district to the north-west, the towns of Mildenhall (8,350) and Brandon (4,545) have grown since 1960 under development schemes. Brandon, the centre of the flint-knapping industry, still supplies gun-flints to the U.S.A., but its principal importance now comes from its association with the vast plantations of the Forestry Commission in this area, much of whose timber goes to the Brandon depot for peeling, and processing into stakes, woodpulp, and pit-props.

In East Suffolk, Stowmarket (9,020), on the A45, is a busy town whose shops and industries cater for

The port of Felixstowe, with the container terminal in the foreground

a wide region. Imperial Chemical Industries have a paint-works here, and Munton and Fison a Queen's Award-winning malt products factory. There is much turkey-rearing in the neighbourhood, and the weekly market is particularly notable for pig sales. Beccles (8,170), in the Waveney Valley, is the home of Clowes, the printers, employing more than a thousand people. Another firm makes high-pressure valve gear for the mining and gas industries, and survival systems for North Sea drilling platforms. The town, on the edge of Broadland, also has a thriving tourist industry: as many as 7,000 boats moor there in the course of a season, and there are boat-building and repairing premises. At Bungay (4,120), also in the Waveney

Valley, another well-known firm of printers – Messrs Clay and Son – have been established since 1876. Leiston-cum-Sizewell (4,920) has one of the largest nuclear power stations of the Central Electricity Generating Board, and there are plans to extend it. One advantage of the 245 acre (100 hectare) seaside site is that 25,000,000 gallons (113,000,000 litres) of sea-water per hour can be used for the cooling system. The old and well-known firm of Garretts (see Chapter 16) no longer makes agricultural implements, but machine tools and wrought ironwork. Other Leiston factories make industrial protective clothing, and Christmas decorations.

70

SUFFOLK EMPLOYMENT STATISTICS: 1973 FIGURES

	Employment Category	Men	Women	Total	%
	EXTRACTIVE				
I	Agriculture, Horticulture, Forestry, and Fishing	10640	3648	14288	6·87
II	Mining/Quarrying	531	42	573	0·28
	TOTAL EXTRACTIVE	**11171**	**3690**	**14861**	**7·15**
	MANUFACTURING				
III	Food, Drink, Tobacco	8761	5793	14554	7·00
IV/V	Chemicals	3398	1389	4787	2·30
VI	Metal Manufacture	1012	162	1174	0·57
VII	Mechanical Engineering	11792	1840	13632	6·56
VIII	Instrument Engineering	693	431	1124	0·54
IX	Electrical Engineering	3019	3871	6890	3·32
X	Shipbuilding and Marine Engineering	2074	146	2220	1·07
XI	Vehicles	3916	529	4445	2·14
XII	Other Metal Goods	1196	337	1533	0·74
XIII	Textiles	793	655	1448	0·70
XIV	Leather and Fur	178	96	274	0·13
XV	Clothing and Footwear	580	2031	2611	1·26
XVI	Bricks, Cement, Pottery, Glass	1161	173	1334	0·64
XVII	Timber, Furniture, Shop/Office Fitting	2911	649	3560	1·71
XVIII	Paper, Printing, Publishing	3509	1654	5163	2·49
XIX	Toys, Stationery, Plastics, Brushes, Sports Equipment	2553	1351	3904	1·88
	TOTAL MANUFACTURING	**47546**	**21107**	**68653**	**33·05**
	SERVICES				
XX	Construction	13308	603	13911	6·70
XXI	Gas, Water, Electricity	3421	806	4227	2·03
XXII	Transport, Communications	11507	1760	13267	6·39
XXIII	Distributive Trades	12204	12545	24749	11·91
XXIV	Insurance, Banking, Finance	3084	3012	6096	2·93
XXV	Professional, Scientific	9100	19634	28734	13·83
XXVI	Miscellaneous Services	9624	11703	21327	10·27
XXVII	Public Administration	8686	3239	11925	5·74
	TOTAL SERVICES	**70934**	**53302**	**124236**	**59·80**
	Unclassified	3	–	3	0·00
	GRAND TOTAL	**129654**	**78099**	**207753**	**100·00**

Mid-Victorian Lowestoft from the pier

CHAPTER 18
SUFFOLK AND THE SEA

It seems inevitable that a county whose coastline is more than 50 miles (80 kilometres) long should have agelong and important associations with the sea.

THE ROMAN PERIOD: SUFFOLK AS PART OF THE SAXON SHORE

The Romans recognized the vulnerability of this coast, part of the Saxon Shore which, in the second half of their four centuries' occupation, was subject to attacks from raiding-parties across the North Sea. Their fleet, the *Classis Britannica*, its sailors wearing blue clothes for camouflage, patrolled the sea, and two of their castles – the forts of the Saxon Shore – stood on the Suffolk coast. One, Gariannonum, or Burgh Castle, is now (since 1974) in Norfolk. The other, at Walton, or Old Felixstowe, has been washed away by the sea. Two centuries ago there were 187 yards (171 metres) of wall left, and a 'great variety of Roman urns, rings, coins, etc.' were found in the area. Early this century nothing remained but a clump of weedy rocks.

THE MIDDLE AGES

In the Prologue to *The Canterbury Tales*, Chaucer, whose father lived in Ipswich as a boy, describes how the merchant:

> . . . wolde the see were kept for anything
> Betwixe Middleburgh and Orewelle.

There was never a town called Orwell: this was the name of the harbour district covering the mouths of the Orwell and Stour estuaries. Ipswich was the real port, rivalling Dunwich, which in 1279 had eighty 'great ships' to Ipswich's thirty. But with the sea's advance, Dunwich declined steadily after the fourteenth century, while Ipswich built up a sizeable merchant fleet during the Middle Ages. Ships left her quays with wool and cloth for Europe. Piracy follows trade, and Suffolk ports were both offenders and victims. Dunwich men attacked a Walberswick ship and murdered sixteen of its crew in 1332. Three years later, four ships, manned by Englishmen, lay in Orwell haven for several months, robbing and sinking trading-ships and holding their crews to ransom. And in 1340, Dunwich and Bawdsey joined their fleets with Great Yarmouth's to attack a Flanders-bound ship, stealing cargo worth £20,000, so that the King himself eventually had to compensate her owners.

THE TUDOR AND STUART PERIODS

One of the most profitable medieval trades was conveying pilgrims to overseas shrines. Ipswich, Woodbridge, and Southwold all participated in this early venture into the tourist industry, now so generally practised by coastal towns. But trade in more material things brought richer rewards. Ships from those same three towns, along with others from Aldeburgh, Thorpe, Sizewell, Dunwich, Walberswick, Covehithe, and Lowestoft, made up the fishing fleet to Iceland in 1528. Ipswich ships brought timber from the Baltic and spices from the Mediterranean. The *Mary Walsingham*, owned by Henry Tooley, an Ipswich merchant and benefactor, was known at Bordeaux: some of her cargo of wine was sent to Lavenham for 'my Lord of Oxford' and to a Lowestoft innkeeper. Books about the 'new learning', those ideas which led to the Reformation, were sometimes imported through east coast ports, hidden in barrels of cargo, to be dispersed throughout the whole country.

Ipswich supplied two ships for the Armada squadron, paying for them by mortgaging the Portmen's Meadow. Aldeburgh was asked for one, with help from five smaller places, and complained that their contributions were negligible. The enthusiasm for battle in Armada year seems not to have been very obvious in Suffolk. But the Elizabethan Age produced some remarkable sailors from these parts. John Eldred, though Norfolk-born, made his fortune in Syria, in the spice trade, and returned to build Nutmeg Hall, at Saxham, near Bury, with the profits. Though the house is gone, his tomb remains in the church. Thomas Eldred, possibly his cousin, sailed with Thomas Cavendish of Trimley, near Felixstowe, the second Englishman to circumnavigate the world: their journey took them through the Magellan Strait, and only fifty men lived to return home in 1588. Sir Martin Stuteville, of Dalham, near Newmarket, went with Drake on his last voyage, and his monument in Dalham Church bears the words (in Latin): 'In his youth he saw America with Francis Drake.' Richard Hakluyt, who recorded all these adventures in his great book, *The Principal Voyages and Discoveries of the English Nation*, was Rector of Wetheringsett.

Henry VIII's Woolwich and Deptford dockyards obtained some of their timber from Suffolk, whose oaks were in demand for their great length and straightness. Phineas Pett, born in 1570, a Chatham shipwright who married a Woodbridge girl, travelled all over the county buying timber for the Navy, and arranging for it to be shipped to the Thames Estuary. One oak tree from Loudham was so large that sixteen horses were needed to drag it to Woodbridge. Suffolk men, too, were valued as sailors on account of their toughness and independent natures.

Naturally, one of the principal activities of the coastal towns was fishing. Aldeburgh was famous for its 'Spratte Fare' in the late autumn: enormous catches were made in Elizabeth's reign. Another curious delicacy was the porpoise: the Corporation of Aldeburgh used to send presents of them to those whose favours and good offices they sought.

John Eldred's bust in Great Saxham Church

Richard Eaton was paid, in 1560, 'for a porpoise for my Lord Mare'. But, at about this same time, troubles began. There were the constant depredations of the Dunkirkers, groups of pirates based at Dunkirk who attacked defenceless shipping. In the uncertain times of the early Stuart period they grew even bolder, bottling up a fleet of fifty-eight Ipswich ships in the Orwell in 1626, and frightening the people of Aldeburgh into repairing some of their dilapidated defences. Another anxiety was increasing competition from the Dutch, whose fishing-boats invaded home waters in their hundreds, after herring. A locally written pamphlet of 1615 praised the courage of the fishermen of Orford, Aldeburgh, Dunwich, and Southwold, but said: 'In all these places the Dutch swim like elephants while we wade like sheep.' A few years later, in 1644, the troubles of the Civil War prompted the Bailiffs and Burgesses of Aldeburgh to petition the Long Parliament: 'Whereas this town is seated right upon the sea and depends much upon the fishing trade, it is now much decayed, as also are all the coast towns of Suffolk. . . .' Things improved, and in 1666 the autumn fishing was particularly prosperous – the sea was 'fuller of herrings than was ever known' – and fishermen were throwing some of their catches back again. By 1670 there were thirty-three boats in the Suffolk fishing fleet.

The seventeenth century also saw a great, if indecisive, sea-battle fought off the Suffolk coast, between the combined English and French fleets and the Dutch. De Ruyter, the Dutch Admiral, with ninety-one ships, surprised 101 English and French ships lying in Sole Bay on 28 May 1672. In the fourteen-hour battle, the French sheered off, leaving James, Duke of York, to fight de Ruyter. We lost six ships, the Dutch three. The gunfire of the battle is said to have been audible as far away as London: what must it have been like in Southwold, where hundreds of people lined the shore to watch? Smoke obscured the whole coast as far south as Essex. Southwold's gardens still yield the occasional cannon-ball from this holocaust.

THE GEORGIAN AGE

The shores of the Orwell produced two notable sailors in the eighteenth century. Admiral Vernon, of Nacton, who in the war against France and Spain captured Portobello in 1739, but who is perhaps better remembered for his instructions to dilute the sailors' rum ration with water: the resulting mixture, called 'grog', was a reference to the Admiral's grogram cloak – a mixture of wool, silk, and mohair. Sir Philip Broke, of Broke Hall, also in Nacton, in his ship *Shannon*, captured the American *Chesapeake* in Boston Harbour in 1813. Nelson's association with Suffolk was a fleeting one. Ipswich honoured him with its High Stewardship, but he disliked the town and, in spite of having a house there (called 'Roundwood', in Victory Road, now replaced by a primary school), he spent only one night there. Sir Thomas Slade, designer of Nelson's flagship, *Victory*, is buried in St Clement's Church, in Ipswich. The war against Napoleon, in which Nelson fought and died, has left a tangible mark on Suffolk in the shape of Martello towers. They were named after a similar structure at Mortella Point, in Corsica, which had successfully resisted attack in an earlier war. A hundred and three of these towers were built, as an anti-invasion measure, round the south and east coasts, eighteen of them in Suffolk. Eleven of these still stand, in varying degrees of repair or dereliction. The Aldeburgh tower was the last in the whole series and, unlike the rest, is shaped like a four-leafed clover. The others are more or less circular, their walls thicker on the seaward side. Some 700,000 bricks were needed for each one: they came by barge from London, and were unloaded directly on to the beach close to the building operations. Each tower was in touch with the next one by semaphore, as well as with beacons and church towers farther inland. In Woodbridge, St Mary's Church had a tar barrel kept ready on its roof, to be fired as a warning to the neighbourhood if news came from the coast that the French had landed. In the twentieth century, similar fears of invasion were entertained in both world wars. As a result, Suffolk's coastal fringes and country lanes are still dotted with curious concrete circular or hexagonal 'pill-boxes', built as look-out posts, scaled-down versions of the Martello towers of a century or more earlier.

LIGHTHOUSES AND LIGHTSHIPS

Other kinds of warning and assistance are provided by the lighthouses, lightships, and lifeboats along the coast. Lowestoft Ness is the most easterly point of the British Isles. Two lights were placed there in 1609, one on the beach, the other on the cliff-top. The lower one, after being moved several times because of the sea's encroachment, was discontinued in 1923. The High Light, still in use, its beam ranging over 14 miles (22·5 kilometres), is open to the public. Farther south, Orfordness Lighthouse with its 99 foot (30 metre) red and white striped tower, is the successor to two lights originally placed there in 1637, probably because ten years earlier thirty-two ships had been lost there in a storm. The inshore passage along Orfordness was used by ships going from northern ports to London, and had become dangerous through silting up. The original structures at Orford were 'timber buildings and very crazy'. After several

Southwold Lighthouse

74

rebuildings the lower one was abandoned altogether and built at Southwold instead. Orford light was made automatic in 1959, monitored over a landline from Harwich. Its beam is visible for 15 miles (24 kilometres). In the First World War it unwittingly helped the German Zeppelins on their bombing raids. Their navigation aids were almost non-existent, so they made for the easily recognizable landmark of the lighthouse, and proceeded from it towards their inland targets.

Lightships are sited where shoals extend well out to sea and might endanger shipping. The best known of them, the *Cork*, off Felixstowe, was replaced in 1975 by a Large Automatic Navigation Buoy (LANBY), with light and fog-signal powered by its own generator. It can operate for six months without attention.

THE LIFEBOAT SERVICE

Before the institution of lifeboats, ships running aground had little chance. In a great storm in 1770, thirty vessels were lost, with all hands, on the Lowestoft sands. In October 1789, forty more ran aground between Great Yarmouth and Southwold in another storm. Two curious structures still standing on Aldeburgh beach today were the 'watch-towers' of the beach companies, the privately owned salvage companies who kept watch there for wrecks. The poet Crabbe, who lived at Aldeburgh, described how they would:

Wait on the shore, and as the waves run high,
On the toss'd vessel bend their eager eye.

The Royal National Lifeboat Institution was founded in 1825. Next year, the Suffolk Shipwreck Association placed a lifeboat at Sizewell which was transferred to Aldeburgh in 1851, the date of the town's first official lifeboat station. A second started in 1905 and lasted until 1959. Between them, Aldeburgh's lifeboats saved more than 500 lives, though not without losses of their own: three lifeboatmen died in 1859, and in 1899 the *Aldeburgh* capsized trying to reach a ship in distress in an easterly gale, and seven of her crew were drowned. The present lifeboat at Aldeburgh stands ready just outside the Jubilee Hall, and can be in the water in a few minutes after a signal-rocket has been fired to call up the crew. Lowestoft's first rescue-boat, a quarter of a century before the R.N.L.I. was founded, was a rowing-boat. A later lifeboat, the *Michael Stephens*, was only one year old when it went to Dunkirk, in 1940, to help with the evacuation of the British Expeditionary Force. In 1959 it took off the crew of a ship which, with a cargo of straw, caught alight off Pakefield. The straw washed overboard stretched for miles along the coast. The present lifeboat, *Frederick Edward*

Crick, is 47 feet (14 metres) long and has twin 60 h.p. diesel engines. Southwold, Kessingland, Pakefield, Thorpeness, Dunwich, and Woodbridge, have all had lifeboats at some time or other. Southwold was chosen in 1896 for a demonstration of launching a lifeboat from an open beach, in the presence of the German Chief Inspector of Lifeboats. The Southwold crews were awarded medals by France in 1905 and Holland in 1911 for rescuing sailors from those countries.

LIFEBOAT STATIONS OF THE R.N.L.I. IN SUFFOLK
(TO 1974)

	Opened	Closed	Lives saved
Aldeburgh No.1	1851	–	510
No.2	1905	1959	51
Corton	1869	1879	3
Dunwich	1873	1903	21
Kessingland No.1	1870	1936	86
No.2	1867	1918	58
No.3	1884	1896	–
Lowestoft No.1	1801	–	726 since 1868
No.2	1869	1913	68
Pakefield No.1	1840	1922	179
No.2	1871	1895	11
Southwold No.1	1841	1940	152
No.2	1866	1920	40
Thorpeness	1853	1900	93
Woodbridge	1801	1853	4

SMUGGLING

A chapter about Suffolk and the sea could not be closed without reference to what was, over long periods, a major local industry. As early as 1224, the people of Orford were being urged to assist the Keeper of the Shore to prevent smuggling. In 1592, the Customs officers at Ipswich complained to Lord Burleigh about the amount of corn and butter being secretly smuggled *out* of the country, to Holland. Smuggling went on, intermittently, all the time, but heavy taxation in the seventeenth century encouraged it and made it profitable, and worth the risk. After the wars of the seventeenth and eighteenth centuries, sailors were demobilized at once, without financial compensation: so, many found it easy to throw in their lot with a gang of smugglers and turn their experience of the sea to their country's disadvantage.

Customs duties increased astronomically from the time of William and Mary. A pound of tea could be bought in Holland for 10p, but the duty on it was more that twice that sum. Brandy was 45p per gallon: smugglers could sell it for 15p and still make a profit. Farm-labourers earning a few pence a day welcomed the chance of being paid £1 a day for carting the goods inland. In 1775, the Parish Clerk of Wingfield was dismissed because of being absent from his duties for three weeks while smuggling! Suffolk's coast was popular because it had good facilities for getting the stuff ashore, often under the eyes of the helpless Revenue officers, who were sometimes bought and sometimes threatened: one at Snape had his nose slit, in 1727, after refusing a bribe. In 1722 it was well known that a recognized tariff existed of the rates of bribes paid to the Revenue men by smugglers, according to the value of the contraband. Such co-operation is not surprising, for neither they nor their families received compensation for death or injury incurred in carrying out their duties.

Smugglers were reported to be 'very numerous' in Ipswich in 1733, 'and so insolent in the town and country that they bid defiance to the officers and threaten their lives'. That same year, Robert Crabbe, the grandfather of the poet, who was Controller of Customs at Aldeburgh, reported that in twelve months he and other officers along the coast had seized 54,000 lb (24,500 kg) of tea and 123,000 gallons (553,000 litres) of brandy, in Essex, Suffolk, and Kent, but he added that 'compared with the total of successful runs, they were sorry figures indeed'. A few years later, in 1745, Admiral Vernon sent the Secretary of the Admiralty some figures: in the second half of that year, he wrote, there had been an estimated 4,551 horseloads of smuggled goods landed and dispersed through the county.

Suffolk is full of so-called 'hiding-places' for smuggled goods. Most coastal villages can tell tales of secret passages, many of which can be rationally explained: they are usually old drains or dried-up wells. But Rishangles Church, a long way inland, is reputed to have sheltered contraband: when repairs were carried out in 1858 a hole was found beneath the pulpit, with the remains of wooden kegs and broken bottles still in it. One Sizewell woman smuggler stored her wares under the platform of the Quakers' meeting-house in Leiston. A load of smuggled tobacco was discovered, on its way to such a shelter, by a Woodbridge landlady who peeped under the cover of a cart in her inn-yard. She fetched the Customs officers, and subsequently used her reward to build a house near by, naming it Tobacco Lodge.

New methods were tried, in the Napoleonic Wars, to prevent such wholesale smuggling. A Preventive Waterguard, established in 1809 to co-operate with the Revenue officers, set up stations, manned by a chief officer, chief boatman, two commissioned boatmen, and four ordinary boatmen. They were issued with one-legged seats (like a shooting-stick) when on watch: if the man fell asleep, he overbalanced. According to an order-book of 1823, dismissals from the service for drunkenness and neglect of duty were frequent: two Lowestoft men lost their jobs this way, and the whole Southwold force was transferred to other stations because of suspicious conduct. The formation of a mixed civilian and naval force in 1829 marked an improvement. Two years later, it became purely naval, under Admiralty control. Legislation in 1856 finalized its organization, and laid the foundations of the later Coastguard Service.

Memorial in Aldeburgh Church to the 1899 lifeboat tragedy

CHAPTER 19
SUFFOLK'S WILDLIFE

In this county largely given over to arable farming, the modern farming methods increasingly applied over the last quarter of a century have inevitably destroyed much of the wildlife's natural habitat. Hedgerows have been uprooted, woodland felled, fens and marshes drained, to create more land for crop-growing. It is fortunate that such organizations as the Royal Society for the Protection of Birds, and the Suffolk Trust for Nature Conservation, have been able to preserve examples of each kind of habitat in their Reserves, ensuring that the associated flora and fauna are not entirely lost.

Hedges support a large proportion of our wildlife: to them we owe the survival of most woodland birds in an agricultural landscape. The number and variety of nests in a hedge depends partly on the number of species and shrubs in it, and a hedge survey can be of great value and interest to the naturalist. It is generally agreed that a hedge 100 years old has only one or two species in a 37 yard (30 metre) stretch; one 200 years old will have two or three species, and so on. The Suffolk Trust has recently acquired its first hedgerow reserve, at Polstead. Dr Max Hooper, who has made a special study of hedges, thinks that this one could be more than 500 years old: there are nineteen species in its 325 yard ((300 metre) length.

The large areas of coniferous forest, planted and maintained by the Forestry Commission on heathland in the east and west of the county, now provide man-made habitats for certain birds and mammals, though they are somewhat limited by the lack of variety in the trees – mainly Scots and Corsican pines.

A summary of the principal kinds of countryside, with the birds, flowers, and mammals found there, follows at the end of this chapter, with a map showing the twenty-nine Reserves of the Suffolk Trust for Nature Conservation. Access to these is available to members of the Trust, whose subscriptions provide most of the funds needed for their upkeep. Information about membership and the work of the Trust may be obtained from the General Secretary, Group Captain F. W. Sledmere, at Osierbed House, Little Bealings, Woodbridge, Suffolk. Corporate membership for schools is available.

MAMMALS

Deer. Four kinds are found in Suffolk: Red, Roe, Fallow, and Muntjac. The county's original wild deer were exterminated long ago by hunting and deforestation, so that those found now are descendants of deer introduced, mostly, by escaping from deerparks. Numbers have increased since the war in those areas planted by the Forestry Commission, whose policy towards them has changed. When the plantations were young and vulnerable, deer were considered as vermin. Now it is possible to maintain a high deer population without damage becoming insupportable. Suffolk had eleven deerparks in 1892, four in 1950. Now only Helmingham and Ickworth have them, but deer travel a good deal, and it is likely that most fair-sized woods in Suffolk have sheltered one or two at a time. Lord Cranbrook reports observing fallow deer at Glemham for short periods in three years out of four.

Roe deer, descended from several pairs introduced from Germany early this century, are common in the brecklands of the west. In 1970, 120 were counted at West Stow and 30 at Mildenhall. *Red deer* are also found in the West Suffolk forests, and another group has been in the Heveningham-Huntingfield district for nearly twenty years. *Fallow deer* are well established in the forests between the Orwell and Alde rivers, in the woods south of Ipswich, and, again, in the West Suffolk forests. They probably come from park herds which have long been dispersed. *Muntjac deer* are small and live singly or in pairs. Because they do not damage trees, they can exist almost unnoticed.

Rabbits. Before 1954, there were rabbits all over Suffolk. The eastern coastal sandy area, with vast expanses of heath, was an undisturbed breeding-ground, and the breck region of the west was similarly infested. On the Elveden Estate, a great clearance campaign killed 128,856 in 1921–22 (an average of more than six per acre). On the 6,500 acres (2,630 hectares) of the Benacre Estate, near Wrentham, 12,479 were killed in 1952–53.

The disease of myxomatosis first appeared in Suffolk in December 1953, near Southwold. By the end of the following year it affected the whole county. The 1955–56 kill on the Elveden Estate was down to 401, and the 1957–58 kill at Benacre was only 9. Isolated colonies survived and bred until caught later by another wave of the disease. Since 1958, rabbit clearance societies have been formed with the aim of controlling the rabbit and other pests, like the coypu and wood-pigeon.

Coypu. This native of South America, bred for its fur, called 'nutria', was introduced into Norfolk in the 1930s, and it is thought that the large number of coypu in East Anglia have all come from some which escaped in the Norwich area in 1937. They are large rat-like creatures, with webbed hind feet and long tails, and two enormous front teeth in each jaw. The average full-grown male is 3 feet (1 metre) long and weighs 30 lb (14 kg). A pair can produce fifty young in a lifetime. They have only reached nuisance proportions since the 1950s, when farmers began to report damage to their crops (especially sugar-beet) and river authorities found river-walls and ditch-banks undermined. The coypu can scratch out earth from under the top edge of a ditch, and tunnel through to the field, causing the bank to collapse and the ditch to block. The Ministry of Agriculture, Fisheries and Food has recognized the problem and encouraged a clearance campaign in coypu-infested territories. Their latest figures show that between 1970 and 1975 13,361 coypu were killed in Suffolk alone.

Squirrels. Red squirrels are widely distributed through the forested areas of both west and east: nibbled pine-cones show where they have been at work. The grey (North American) squirrel invaded the south and south-west of the county in 1955–60 and rapidly increased. In 1969, a vermin-shoot at Rougham, near Bury, killed 106 of them. In 1973, 400 were shot at the same place, which gives an idea of the extent to which the nuisance has increased.

Other mammals. Badgers have colonized Forestry Commission plantations in the west. Moles are common, particularly on the sandy soils. The number of foxes has increased in recent years. Bank- and field-voles, and the long-tailed field-mouse are common everywhere, but harvest mice, which used to nest in cornfields, are being discouraged by modern agricultural methods: however, there are still plenty in marshes and reed-beds. The pipistrelle bat is common throughout Suffolk: large colonies breed in old houses, barns, or churches. Well-wooded areas shelter the long-eared bat, and the lesser horseshoe bat has been recorded in the Bury area.

REPTILES, AMPHIBIANS, AND FISH
There are adders and common lizards on the sandy heathlands, especially on the edges of forest areas. Grass-snakes are found mainly near marshes and rivers, from which they get tadpoles and tiny fish to eat. All parts of Suffolk have frogs and toads, though many are killed on the roads. Pike, perch, roach, rudd, and bream are the most generally found coarse fish in Suffolk rivers.

BUTTERFLIES AND MOTHS
Because conditions in the countryside have changed since the war in the ways described at the beginning of this chapter, the total number of butterflies has decreased. Part of the blame is frequently put on the increasing use of chemical sprays, but there is no evidence to support this. It may be true to say that the number of wayside flowers has been reduced, but plenty remain for butterflies to feed on. Some species which are scarce in Suffolk (for example the large tortoiseshell and purple emperor) were never common, and were usually confined to particular woods where sprays were not used. Climatic changes are more likely to affect insects: a cool summer when they are active could reduce the numbers of scarcer species without affecting the common, widely spread ones. Some species vary from one decade to another, and it is possible that some which appear to have gone from Suffolk may return at a future time.

The commoner butterflies are still very common: hedge brown, meadow brown, small and large skipper, small, large, and green-veined white, common and holly blue, small copper, small tortoiseshell, peacock, and comma. The presence of the red admiral, painted lady, and clouded yellow depends on immigration from abroad in the early summer months.

The cinnabar moth, whose black and yellow caterpillars feed on ragwort, is the most common Suffolk moth. Five more are wholly, or almost wholly, confined to the area around Mildenhall: the viper's bugloss, grey carpet, spotted sulphur, tawny wave, and diamond-spot pearl moths. Another group is found mainly in conifer plantations or scattered pine-clumps. These are the pine hawk moth (whose caterpillars feed on pine-needles), pine shoot moth (which can damage the shoots of young trees and cause deformed growth), the pine beauty, pine carpet, grey pine carpet, and bordered white moths. Many more are associated with coast and marsh vegetation along the seashore, including the wainscot moths which feed on grasses.

BIRDS
Suffolk is on one of the main bird migration-routes in Britain. The coastline, regular and open, has none of those features – prominent headlands and isolated islands – which, in other parts, provide favourable points for observing migratory move-

ments. In spite of this it has been rightly said that
the Suffolk coast can probably show as much
migration as any maritime county in England. The
main movements which may be observed are these:

The arrival and departure of summer migrants.

The arrival and departure of winter visitors.

Waders on passage to their breeding-areas.

Drift migrants (when night migrants from
Scandinavia, crossing Britain in autumn, en-
counter headwinds or rain and are forced to land.
Conditions like these produce great migratory
'rushes' to our coast, filling the fields and hedges
with redstarts or robins or goldcrests).

East European vagrants in autumn.

Irruption of species such as crossbill and
waxwing: on 27 January 1950, a flock of a hundred
waxwings came in from the sea over Orfordness.

Overshooting by birds in the spring, when
moving west or north-west.

American species which have been blown off-
course.

Hard-weather movements and sea-bird movements. Gannets, Manx shearwaters, great and
Arctic skuas, kittiwakes, puffins, fulmars, and
razorbills are usually seen inshore only when driven
in by hard weather and an onshore wind.
Sometimes, in especially severe conditions, there are
'wrecks' when sea-birds are driven well inland. Birds
such as the guillemot are sometimes driven inshore
when they become oiled.

Winter visitors. These come from the cold regions
to the north, north-west, and east of the British
Isles. Snow covers their breeding-grounds for long
periods, so they move to the milder maritime parts
of western Europe, where the winter snow is
comparatively short-lived. Birds display a remarkable precision in migration: some return regularly
to the same small area of territory, and ringed birds
have been recorded passing through the same
locality on the same date in consecutive years.

Brent geese visit our coast and estuaries in small
numbers at certain times of the winter. In 1976,
about 150 roosted on the Deben's lower reaches and
spent the day feeding on fields behind the river-wall.
Wigeon, teal, pintail, shelduck, and mallard feed on
the estuary mudflats. On the shoreline, it is possible
to find twite and snow bunting feeding on the seeds
of vegetable matter left on the tideline or in the
shingle. The shorelark is rarer, since 1955, and is a
casual visitor only in very small numbers.

Large numbers of wading birds winter on our
estuaries: knot, redshank, grey plover, black-tailed
godwit, and dunlin. Ten thousand of the last-named
species were counted on the Orwell one January,
and up to a thousand have been seen on the Deben
mudflats at Waldringfield. The purple sandpiper
comes in small numbers to areas where old

Teal, a winter visitor to Suffolk's estuaries

breakwaters and shingle-banks provide conditions
it likes. The sanderling, as its name suggests, prefers
wide, sandy beaches, though one small flock has
wintered regularly on the harbour-walls at
Lowestoft.

A few birds of prey come to winter here: rough-
legged buzzards and hen harriers in the forests and
heaths, peregrine falcons and merlins on the coastal
grazing marshes. The merlin preys on smaller
wading birds, but has even been seen chasing
blackbirds, swifts, and redwings. The marsh harrier
returned to Suffolk only at about the time of the
Second World War. Its breeding-site at Minsmere
is the only one in Britain, apart from one or two
occasional isolated instances outside the Reserve.

Large numbers of fieldfare and redwing arrive
from the Continent from September on. In mild
weather they may stay here, but they usually pass on
westwards fairly quickly.

The avocet in Suffolk. In April 1947, after a century
in which this species had not been known to nest
successfully in Britain, four pairs of avocets nested
on flooded marshes at Minsmere. In July, four more
pairs were discovered on Havergate Island. Soon
afterwards, the island was acquired by the R.S.P.B.,
and the colony increased each year: there were
twenty-two pairs in 1950 and sixty-seven pairs by
1960. At Minsmere, however, they only resumed
breeding in 1963 after an area called a 'scrape' was
planned, to provide a safer nesting and feeding

Avocets at one of the R.S.P.B. Reserves

environment for birds, including the avocets, whose existence was increasingly affected by human activity. Predators are controlled there, though rats occasionally manage to get in, and a fox once destroyed six clutches of avocet eggs.

The avocet is one of the first summer visitors to arrive: as early as February in 1975, in a mild spell, though March is more usual. One or two have even been known to spend the winter at Minsmere or in Butley Creek. They are aggressive birds and, at Minsmere, have forced mute swans and Canada geese to withdraw. Avocet chicks show the same aggression when only ten days old.

Reserves managed by the Royal Society for the Protection of Birds. (1) *Minsmere Bird Reserve*, on the Suffolk coast about two miles south of Dunwich, is one of the most important reserves belonging to the R.S.P.B. and covers 1,560 acres (630 hectares) of a wide variety of habitat. It includes freshwater reedbeds, open meres, sand-dunes, seashore, heathland, woodland, and the famous 'scrape', a man-made area of shallow brackish water where twenty species of bird breed successfully: the avocets and three species of sea tern are the most notable.

The reedmarsh, where the rare marsh harriers breed, was formed after land north of the New Cut was flooded in 1940 as part of the wartime coastal defence scheme. By the end of the war, reeds had spread from the ditches and decoy-pools into the lower flooded fields and reed-fringed shallow meres.

As a result of protection, and new management methods, there are now 100 species breeding on this reserve.

(2) *Havergate Island* in the estuary of the River Ore, two miles downstream from the village of Orford, consists mainly of 280 acres (113 hectares) of saltmarsh. The R.S.P.B. acquired the Reserve in 1947 after avocets were found breeding there. They continue to breed successfully. The Reserve is also noted for its winter wildfowl population, the waders which pass through on passage in spring and autumn, and birds like the short-eared owl which also breed there.

Bird exhibitions. Suffolk has two collections of stuffed birds: there is a varied collection at Moyses Hall Museum, Bury St Edmunds, and the fine Ogilvie Collection at Ipswich Museum, housed in 235 habitat cases, and presented in 1918. It includes the now extinct British great bustard, which once roamed over the West Suffolk Breckland.

SOME EXAMPLES OF HABITAT IN SUFFOLK

Woodland – Staverton Forest and Staverton Thicks (Eyke-Butley), woods around Bentley, Groton Wood, Combs Wood, Bull's Wood (Cockfield), Euston.
Birds: Marsh and willow tit, redstart, willow warbler, blackbird, hawfinch, nuthatch, blue tit, great tit, coal tit, robin, treecreeper, sparrowhawk, woodcock.

The Military (or Soldier) Orchid

Flowers: Herb paris, dog's mercury, primrose, wood anemone, bluebell, early purple orchid, butterfly orchid, common spotted orchid, oxlip, violet helleborine, spurge laurel, wood sorrel.
Fungi: Death-Cap (*Amanita phalloides*) is more common in the woods of East Anglia (especially oak and beech) than anywhere else.
Mammals: Dormouse, grey squirrel, bank vole, shrew, badger, fox, woodmouse.

Coniferous forest – Dunwich, Rendlesham, Tunstall, West Stow (King's Forest).
Birds: Coal tit, goldcrest, redpoll, great spotted woodpecker, crossbill, long-eared owl, chaffinch, robin, blackbird, wren.
Flowers: An acid soil and accumulations of pine-needles under densely planted trees preclude the growth of plants, but in the wide forest 'rides' and between young trees one can sometimes find heathland flowers and plants. There is a stream flowing through Rendlesham Forest, with waterside plants. Bracken and bramble grow under trees where light penetrates the canopy of foliage.
Fungi: In abundance – agaric and boletus are very common.
Mammals: Red deer, roe deer, fallow deer, red squirrel.

Heathland – Breckland, Cavenham Heath, Hollesley Heath and Common, Tuddenham (Barton Mills), Blaxhall Common, Rushmere Heath, Tunstall Common, Westleton Heath.

Birds: Red-backed shrike, nightjar, woodlark, tree pipit, linnet, stone curlew, stonechat, yellow hammer, whitethroat.
Flowers: Ling, bell heather, gorse, broom, bracken, heath spotted orchid.
Mammals: Rabbit.
Reptiles: Adder, common lizard.

Fens, Marshes, and Reedbeds – Coastal marshes from Dunwich to Walberswick, Minsmere Level, Redgrave and Lopham Fens, Tuddenham Fen, Westwood Marsh (Walberswick), area between Sudbourne and Hollesley.
Birds: Marsh harrier, bittern, bearded tit (all especially important), reed warbler, sedge warbler, Savi's warbler, grasshopper warbler, snipe, redshank, meadow pipit, yellow wagtail.
Flowers: Fen orchid (rare), southern marsh orchid, marsh sow thistle, marsh helleborine, ragged robin, great willowherb, common reed, reedmace, butterwort, grass of Parnassus.
Mammals: Coypu, otter, stoat.
Reptiles: Grass-snake.
The rare Large Raft Spider (*Dolomedes plantarius*) is found in the Redgrave and Lopham Fens S.T.N.C. Reserve.

Saltmarsh – Alde Estuary, Blyth, Deben, Orwell, Butley Creek, Havergate Island.
Birds: Avocet, redshank, black-headed gull.
Flowers: Sea lavender, sea purslane, sea aster, sea arrow grass, thrift, samphire, marsh mallow.

Shingle – Benacre Ness, Orfordness, Dunwich to Walberswick, Shingle Street.

The Fritillary (Fritillaria meleagris), *one of Suffolk's rare wild flowers*

Birds: Ringed plover, little tern, common tern, Sandwich tern, wheatear, black-headed gull, oystercatcher.
Flowers: Herb Robert, viper's bugloss, sea rocket, sea bindweed, couch grass, curled dock, sea pea, sea campion, yellow horned poppy, yellow stonecrop, English stonecrop.
Mammals: Rabbit, brown hare.

Sand-dune – Minsmere Beach, Benacre, Sizewell, Walberswick Beach.
Flowers: Marram grass, sea holly, birdsfoot trefoil, rest-harrow, sea couchgrass.

Grassland – Mickfield Meadow, Rookery Farm (Monewden), Gromford Meadow (Snape), and other S.T.N.C. reserves.
Birds: Skylark, meadow pipit.
Flowers: Early purple and green-winged orchids, fritillary, bee orchid, cowslip, autumn crocus, adder's tongue, hayrattle, twayblade.
Mammals: Field vole, mole.

Hedgerow – throughout Suffolk.
Birds: Dunnock, yellowhammer, blackbird, robin, lesser whitethroat.

Flowers: Hawthorn, bramble, greater stitchwort, cow parsley, hedge parsley, lesser celandine, bluebell, alexander (near sea).
Mammals: Bank vole, shrew, stoat, weasel, hedgehog, fox.

Freshwater margins – Rivers Waveney, Stour, Gipping, Alde, Blyth, and Benacre Broad.
Birds: Mute swan, mallard, coot, moorhen, gadwall, garganey, shoveller, great-crested grebe, little crebe, heron (mostly in trees near fresh water, though there are heronries near the Deben and Alde estuaries).
Flowers: Common reed, reedmace, purple loosestrife, yellow loosestrife, water mint, meadow rue, hemp agrimony, yellow flag, sedge (various species), great willowherb, water forget-me-not, greater spearwort, water violet.
Mammals: Water vole, otter, coypu.

Two rare wild flowers grow in the Rex Graham Reserve of the Suffolk Trust for Nature Conservation which is jointly managed by the Trust and the Forestry Commission. These are the military orchid and the Daphne Mezereum: both grow on chalk, and the Reserve is in a pit cut through the sandy topsoil to the underlying chalk.

RESERVES OF THE SUFFOLK TRUST FOR NATURE CONSERVATION

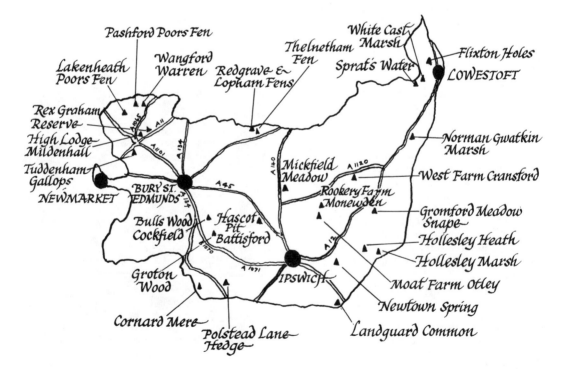

CHAPTER 20
BUILDING MATERIALS AND HISTORIC HOUSES

The absence of local stone has not produced mediocrity or lack of variety in Suffolk's buildings. Beautiful effects of pattern and texture have been obtained by the use of flints – hard, shiny, grey and black stones, formed in the vast chalk-beds that underlie the whole of East Anglia and come to the surface all along the west side. Prehistoric people made them into tools and weapons. Medieval craftsmen used them in building, and builders down to our own day have gone on doing so. The town of Brandon, in north-west Suffolk, illustrates well the use of flint in Suffolk, and provides interesting examples from all periods. Whole villages in that area, like Wangford, Icklingham, and Eriswell, shine with the rich dark flints which occur locally.

The simplest way of using flints is roughly, just as they are, unfractured, producing a ragged but pleasant texture. A number of Suffolk's forty-two round church-towers are built this way. A round tower was a good way of overcoming the absence of limestone for square corners. The flints were set in mortar, and, because plenty of time had to be allowed for hardening, only 10 feet (3 metres) were

built each year: so a 70 foot (20 metre) tower was built over six or seven years, and sometimes seems to have taken a good deal longer still.

A more striking, sparkling effect was achieved if the flints were knapped: this means that they were struck and split, exposing the grey-black surface inside the flint nodule, or lump; then they were shaped and polished. Where knapped flints are used with stone, as in many churches, the resulting mixture is called 'flushwork'. The walls of Gipping Church provide perhaps the most brilliant example of decorative flintwork in Suffolk. Lavenham, Long Melford, Blythburgh, Southwold, and Eye are among the finest of the others, but even small village churches sometimes boast a flushwork porch or parapet of great beauty. Stratford St Mary has Latin and English inscriptions, and the complete alphabet, in limestone and flint, on its village church.

Where the underlying chalk reaches the sea, flints have been dislodged and washed into smooth oval pebbles, called 'kidney cobbles'. They were easily gathered, graded into approximately equal sizes, and used for building, expecially in coastal areas. Lowestoft and Aldeburgh have good examples of houses and walls made of such cobbles.

As described in Chapter 1, two other building materials occur near the coast. One is the Coralline Crag, shelly in texture, which provided the 'stone' for Chillesford and Wantisden church-towers. The other, Septaria, the muddy stone found in the London Clay, crops out along the coast south of Orfordness. With weathering it mellows to a soft grey-brown. Many churches in that part of Suffolk between the Stour and Alde estuaries have some in their towers: Erwarton and Harkstead, for instance. The keep of Orford Castle is largely built of Septaria, and it can be found in the skirting-walls of Framlingham Castle, too. Another small castle, called 'Little Wenham Hall' (a few miles south-west of Ipswich), the best-preserved thirteenth-century house in England, has Septaria in its lower stages. Another of Little Wenham's claims to fame is that the pale yellow and pink bricks of which it is built are some of the earliest used in England since Roman times.

Apart from this, most of Suffolk's brick buildings are of the sixteenth century and later. A number of

Eye: flushwork in the church-tower

Ipswich: the Tudor mansion in Christchurch Park

churches have brick towers: that of Grundisburgh is especially distinguished. Ashbocking's is patterned with diaper-work, where dark bricks are introduced into the red ones, to obtain a criss-cross effect, an idea early put into practice in the Netherlands. Brick was used in domestic buildings, too. On the banks of the Orwell stands the curious six-storeyed Freston Tower. Many fanciful tales claim to explain it, but perhaps the most likely is that it was built by an Ipswich merchant who wanted to watch his ships coming home up the river. In Ipswich, Christchurch Mansion Museum is an E-shaped house of 1548: Elizabeth stayed there in 1561, while she was visiting the town. In the late seventeenth century its porch was given a more Classical appearance and its gables were given curved Flemish shapes. Dutch influence was strong in East Anglia at that time, and a number of buildings in Suffolk were built with these easily recognizable gables. The Dutch were even more dependent on brick than the East Anglians and earlier learnt its uses. There is a spectacular example on the Shire Hall in Woodbridge, but the Waveney Valley has the greatest concentration. Among many good examples in Beccles, one in particular resembles a true Dutch house, with its tall narrow façade rising straight out of the street. Another brick feature that seems to have come to us from the Netherlands is the crinkle-crankle wall (also known as 'ribbon' or 'serpentine' wall). The shelter its curves gave to fruit trees made it popular for kitchen gardens. There are more than fifty in Suffolk: Heveningham Hall has a fine one, but they were not restricted to big houses – good examples can be seen in the streets of Eye, Easton, and Long Melford.

In the west of the county, the Woolpit kilns produced, from the seventeenth century to our own,

'a very white and durable kind of brick' (White's *Directory* of 1844). Many houses and cottages in the Bury–Stowmarket area were built of them: so is Hengrave Hall, near Bury, built 1525–38 for a London merchant, Thomas Kytson, whose arms are flamboyantly displayed over the main entrance.

More than 10,000 buildings in Suffolk are 'listed' by the Department of the Environment, showing that they are important for historic or architectural reasons. A high proportion of them are timber-framed. The frame of the house was built of great oak posts and beams, held together with wooden pegs, which would not rust and split the wood. It has been calculated that in one average-sized prosperous yeoman farmhouse at Stanton, near Bury, $332\frac{1}{2}$ trees were used. The spaces between posts were filled with interwoven hazel twigs, and covered with mud and clay to dry to a solid wall: this was called 'wattle and daub'. Such a clay wall needed protection from the weather, to stop it from being washed out again, and the timbers likewise needed protection, so the whole building was coated with lime-plaster to render it weatherproof and draughtproof. Robert Ryece's *Breviary of Suffolk*, written at the end of the Elizabethan Age, describes and recommends the process: '. . . he doth very well to . . . fill his wide panels . . . with clay or culm enough well-tempered; over which it may be some, of more ability both for warmth, continuance and comeliness, do bestow a cast of hair lime and sand, made into mortar and laid thereon, rough or smooth as the owner pleaseth.'

Large areas of plaster could be covered with a decoration called 'pargework', or 'pargetting', and this craft is particularly associated with East Anglia. There were various methods. The simplest was to use a pointed stick, or bunch of sticks, to trace, or 'comb', a geometrical pattern in the wet

(Opposite) The attractive texture of rough flints: Ramsholt church-tower

Africa, with crocodile and sunshade, in pargetting, on the Ancient House, Ipswich. Charles II's royal arms were added after the Restoration

plaster. Another was to use a simple wooden mould which, when pressed against the plaster, produced a regular design. One house at Clare is covered with a simple and pretty leaf and flower pattern. The most remarkable example in the whole county is in Ipswich itself, where the Ancient House bookshop in the Butter Market has representations of four of the continents under its windows: Australia had yet to be discovered when the work was done in about 1670.

In towns especially, the main corner-post of a wooden-framed house was often ornamented with carvings, and a decorated horizontal beam, or bressumer, inserted over a principal window, or along the 'jettied' angle of an 'over-sailing' house. Ipswich once had many handsome houses with these features. Most have disappeared, but Christchurch Mansion Museum retains a good collection of their corner-posts and bressumers, rescued when the houses themselves were demolished, and preserved as part of the town's history. Suffolk's best examples of timber buildings are to be seen in Lavenham, whose streets are lined with them. Kersey, Hadleigh, Bildeston,

Debenham, and Coddenham all have fine examples. In this century it has become fashionable to remove the plaster coat and expose the timber studwork. Those who do this, not understanding the reason for the plaster, boast that they are 'restoring' their house to its original appearance.

ROOF COVERINGS

Thatch is the oldest and most attractive covering for roofs: nearly twenty Suffolk churches are still thatched, and a 1960 survey by the Rural Community Council concluded that this county had more thatched buildings than any other. Reeds made the best roof, but they were the most expensive and the most difficult to use. They grow at the edges of tidal estuaries in Suffolk, and Butley Church was last rethatched in the early 1960s with locally grown reeds, but the best ones come from the Norfolk Broads and marshes. A reed thatch can last from sixty to a hundred years. It is less subject to attacks from birds or mice, and, not being loose, should not need that protective wire covering usually fastened over a straw thatch. Of the straws, rye is the strongest, but Suffolk roofs are more usually thatched with wheat straw, which can last thirty years: 'Eclipse' is the best variety. Combine-harvesters crush the straw and make it useless for thatching, so it must be cut specially, which adds to the cost of the work. The ridge is the most important and vulnerable part of any roof, needing additional strengthening. Sometimes a straw thatch is given a ridge of reeds, whose lower edges are usually finished off with an elaborate decoration, perhaps of scallops, depending on the art of the thatcher.

Pantiles were made in Suffolk brick-kilns throughout the eighteenth and nineteenth centuries: they are S-shaped in section, to give a deep curve off which the rain could run. A pantiled roof has a rhythmic wavy line to it, and often looks larger and richer than it is. Like the curved gables, pantiles were a Dutch fashion: they were not produced here before 1701. They are usually red, though almost-black ones were made, and used mostly in coastal areas, giving the roof a beautiful shine as they reflected the sky. Glazing the tiles, to strengthen them and reduce the danger from frost, was not common before this century.

SOME SUFFOLK BUILDINGS, FROM NORMAN TIMES TO OUR OWN

Moyses Hall, now the Bury St Edmunds' museum, and built about 1180, is the oldest house in Suffolk. Its ground floor was an undercroft, or storeroom. Above are the original hall and solar, or sitting-room, where the owners could enjoy more privacy. The house looks suspiciously new for its age. This is because it was too thoroughly 'restored' in 1858. Two other spectacular Norman buildings in the county are the castles of Orford and Framlingham (see Chapter 9).

At Framlingham, the finest remains are the skirting-walls, enclosing an oval-shaped space, with flanking towers all round. The private rooms and chapel of the Bigod earls who owned it were originally built against the north-east side of the wall: you can see window-openings, remains of fireplaces, and holes where the beams that supported the flooring were once fixed. In the twelfth and thirteenth centuries, the life of the castle went on inside these great walls: you crossed the moat and came through the gate, rather as though entering a walled and gated town. Framlingham later passed to the Howard dukes of Norfolk, who added the ornamental chimneys for decoration, but preferred the greater comfort of their other houses. In 1655 it was bought by Sir Robert Hitcham who pulled down all but the stone buildings, and made almshouses and a school inside the walls: these are the buildings you see now, and through which you pass to climb to the wall walk.

Orford, built for Henry II in 1165–73, was more up to date and comfortable. The keep (all that remains) has one large room on each of its three floors, while in the three turrets there are a chapel and smaller rooms for greater privacy and comfort.

Little Wenham Hall, already referred to, is the earliest brick house, of the late thirteenth century. With its main hall, chapel, and single upstairs chamber, it would have been cosily domestic compared with Orford or Framlingham, a house rather than a castle, in spite of its battlemented roof.

It used to be thought that Suffolk had no surviving timber-framed houses earlier than the fifteenth century, but in the 1960s and 1970s a number of examples have been found of fourteenth-century 'aisled halls'. One, Edgar's Farmhouse, has been removed to the Museum of East Anglian Life at Stowmarket where it may be seen by the public. The aisled hall was a barn-like structure: the posts supporting the roof could be used to create recesses for privacy. Smoke from the central fire blackened the topmost beams and carved posts as it found its way out of a hole in the roof. Chimneys were a sixteenth-century innovation in houses: the new brick houses of that period incorporated them.

Christchurch Mansion, in Ipswich, is a good

Freston Tower, on the Orwell

87

example of a brick house of the Tudor period. The E-shape is related to the requirements of the time. The heart of the house was still the hall, that central room where most of the everyday life was lived. At one end of this, you had a wing where food was stored and prepared – kitchen, pantry, and buttery – and where the servants lived and worked. At the opposite end, you had the family's private apartments. The pattern could be extended or enlarged, but even in the greatest mansions of that time, the hall remained the principal room, as at Long Melford Hall, basically a house of the 1550s, with Georgian turrets and additions. And in Ipswich, the Ancient House was originally open to its hammer-beam roof, until a later owner cut it in half horizontally, inserted a floor to make a separate upper storey, and panelled the walls to make them warmer and more comfortable. This conversion of a 'hall house' into a normal two-storey one happened quite often in the sixteenth century.

The Georgian period, when young men travelled in Europe on the 'Grand Tour', to complete their education, has left Suffolk a perfect building in the Palladian style: Heveningham Hall. It was designed for Sir Gerard Vanneck, son of a wealthy London merchant, by Sir Robert Taylor, who already had to his credit several country-houses, part of the Bank of England, and some of the monuments in Westminster Abbey. The rooms were decorated by James Wyatt, and they achieve the effect of appearing beautiful, graceful, and grand without seeming cold and formal, like the state rooms in many other ostentatious mansions. A young Frenchman, François de la Rochefoucauld, making

his own Grand Tour in England, in 1784, described Heveningham Hall as 'magnificent – the only one in Suffolk really worth seeing'. He especially admired the dining-room: 'I have never seen anything to compare with the perfect proportions of this room or with the elegance of its decoration. Its dimensions are thirty-two feet by twenty-four, and three very broad windows let in magnificent light.' This room was burnt out in 1949, but restored according to the original plans, which fortunately had been kept.

The stables and park at Heveningham are the work of Lancelot Brown, better known as 'Capability' Brown from his sensible habit of saying, when asked his opinion of a garden, that he saw 'capability of improvement'. In front of the mansion he planted trees, and created the lake from a series of nondescript ponds, to provide suitable Romantic views from the windows along the main front.

De la Rochefoucauld was a quarter of a century too early to see Suffolk's other great Georgian house at Ickworth, a mile or two outside Bury. Frederick, Earl of Bristol and Bishop of Derry, began building it about 1794, with Francis Sandys as his architect. The plan of the house is a central rotunda, from which, on either side, a long curved arm leads to a large rectangular pavilion. The Earl-Bishop's intention was to live in the rotunda and use the wings to house his collection of paintings and sculpture, but while he was building up his collection in Italy it was confiscated by Napoleon and he died without ever seeing his house finished. The family did not move in until 1830: even then, much remained to be done, and work went on all through the century. The original scheme was reversed, so that the east wing provided living-quarters, the west wing became a winter garden, and the rotunda was furnished as a series of state rooms. Most of Ickworth now belongs to the National Trust, so its furniture, paintings, and silver may be seen by everyone. It is one of the most extraordinary houses in the whole country.

The early part of Victoria's reign saw some pleasing initial experiments in town-planning in Ipswich. In the 1840s, when the original museum was built, a number of simple, dignified, grey-brick houses were built in what is still called Museum Street (though the institution itself has moved), where there had been nothing before. This was the moment when the town began its nineteenth-century expansion, spreading beyond its medieval boundaries. In the next decade, Fonnereau Road was built, its large Italianate houses looking over the town and Christchurch Park. But the Victorian tastes epitomized by the Great Exhibition of 1851 were insinuating themselves. Some of those houses, the later ones, have friezes and decorated courses of

Heveningham Hall

(Opposite) Ickworth: the Rotunda

coloured tiles, and rather too much ornamental work in stone and iron. By the 1860s, Ipswich had stretched out to the east and west. It is an interesting exercise, generally possible in any sizeable town, to go out along one of the main roads from the town, noticing how the style of the houses becomes more ornate as the nineteenth century advances. If the buildings themselves are mostly undated, a clue is sometimes given in their names, or in the names of the streets in which they stand. Alma Cottages and Inkerman Terrace, for the period of the Crimean War (1854–55), Sedan Street (the Franco-Prussian War of 1870–71), and Jubilee Villa (1887) are some typical examples.

Lloyds Bank buildings in Felixstowe, Ipswich, and Woodbridge, the Westminster Bank and the Crown and Anchor Hotel in Ipswich, and Harvest House (the former Felix Hotel) at Felixstowe, are all the work of a notable architect of the Late Victorian and Edwardian period, T. W. Cotman. The development of Lowestoft and Felixstowe as seaside resorts led to some attractive examples of good 'seaside' architecture there, some of them at Felixstowe only recently demolished in the interests of car-parking. But, in general, over the period, most of the housing was undistinguished in design, and is particularly obtrusive in the countryside. A few landowners have designed agreeable 'estate' villages: at Woolverstone and Somerleyton, around Dalham, and in the Helmingham district.

Since the Second World War, the new cottage-building at Rushbrooke was really an enlightened 'estate' village, built by Lord Rothschild, but unfortunately in materials and of a design more suited to the highland zone of Britain than to East Anglia: slate roofs and whitewashed walls. Some successful council-housing has been managed since the war, for example at Melton, but much seems out of place in our villages, and so does much of the private speculative development, particularly those houses built out of a mixture of materials: brick, stucco, weather-boarding, pebble-dash, and tile-hanging can sometimes all be found in one bungalow! Messrs Tayler and Green of Lowestoft have executed a handful of works in Suffolk – a public house and an old people's complex at Lowestoft, and a similar attractive complex at Woodbridge – but there is nothing here to compare with their admirable enhancement of the former Rural District of Loddon, just over the Norfolk border. In these uninspiring circumstances, sensible caring people in Suffolk support the efforts of local authorities and the Suffolk Preservation Society to conserve the best of those 10,000 listed buildings which constitute the most valuable stock of housing in the community.

Hintlesham Hall. Chimneys (and red-brick garden front) reveal the Tudor house. The handsome Palladian stuccoed mask is early eighteenth century. Fashionable Georgian improvement of Tudor houses is especially characteristic of Suffolk town-building in, for example, Beccles, Bury St Edmunds, and even Lavenham

CHAPTER 21
LOCAL GOVERNMENT

Woodbridge Shire Hall, with curved Dutch gables, stands on the Market Hill

If the long traditions of local government in Suffolk are not widely understood, the fault may lie in their complexity but not in their lack of interest. Indeed, nothing concerns us more closely; but our involvement in such affairs is nowadays much less direct than in former centuries, and policy-making and administration on committees is usually left to salaried officials.

At the lowest range, our parishes, which once had the basic police responsibilities, to say nothing of overseeing the poor and surveying the highways, are now restricted to such matters as allotments, the signposting of footpaths, and (with certain qualifications) burial-grounds. For many centuries, the main communities of higher authority than the parish were the *Shire* (the Old English word for

county), and its subdivision, the *Hundred*, each with its own court, and public functions which touched everybody, especially anyone owning land. At the time of 'Domesday Book', there were twenty-four of these districts of 'Hundredal' administration in Suffolk, and this at once shows that each was closer to the individual member of the community than any of the Districts created in 1974 can ever be, since there are only seven of them to cover and cope with the whole county. The hundred was a reasonably compact group of parishes, almost a neighbourhood, with a working knowledge of its inhabitants and a real community of interests, but the present district is apt to be far-flung: the Suffolk Coastal District stretches from Felixstowe right up to Walberswick, the Mid-Suffolk District from Rattlesden to Mendham, and the St Edmundsbury District from Haverhill to Euston. Furthermore, the shire, or county, in Suffolk was never anything like so large and unwieldy a unit as it became after the 1974 reorganization. For in that year, the single county of Suffolk was created out of *three* previous counties: East Suffolk, West Suffolk, and the County Borough of Ipswich. Those three, established by the previous reorganization of 1888, took the place of the earlier shires into which Suffolk has been divided since the Late Anglo-Saxon period. One of them, known as the 'Liberty of St Edmund', had precisely the same boundaries as the pre-1974 County of West Suffolk. The recent County of East Suffolk had been amalgamated in 1888 from two previous units. One was known as the 'Liberty of St Etheldreda' (an ancient cluster of hundreds grouped about the Deben and Alde rivers). The other bore the ancient title of the 'Geldable' because only those particular hundreds in all Suffolk paid tax (geld) to the sheriff and were subject to his royal jurisdiction. This relative lack of work for the sheriff in Suffolk presumably explains why Suffolk and Norfolk shared one sheriff, successively, from the beginning of Henry II's reign (1154) until the middle of Elizabeth I's reign (1575). In the two liberties, the role of sheriff was played respectively by the Abbot of St Edmund's and the Bishop of Ely.

The complexity of local government in medieval Suffolk was, of course, extended by the relative independence of ancient royal boroughs like Ipswich, and seigneurial boroughs like Sudbury,

Eye, and Bungay. (We saw in Chapter 8 how Ipswich received its Charter from King John in 1200.) The realities of such independence were much reduced from time to time when over-mighty barons or kings pressed too hard. But, in general through elaborately recorded acts and precedents of the borough courts, such important rights as those of married women to property, and of minors to various safeguards, seem to have been established in Ipswich rather earlier and more surely than they were in the Liberties and Geldable.

There were, of course, famous abuses, of which Sudbury's have become celebrated, with the inner ring of freemen excluding all but their friends from effective local government and, in 1771 for instance, finding themselves besieged for ten hours in their own town hall in 'infinite terror and dismay'. We should perhaps be glad that that degree of feeling has largely gone out of local government, but even that kind of feeling is preferable to boredom and apathy.

Between 1888 and 1974, Suffolk's local authorities achieved much to be proud of. The County Borough of Ipswich was one of the first authorities to consider the provision of council-housing: as early as 1913, plans were made for an estate (on Hadleigh Road) to cater for an influx of workmen, but the outbreak of war next year meant postponing them until 1919. After that, Ipswich pursued an energetic programme of slum clearance, rehousing displaced families on large well-conceived estates at Whitton and in the Nacton area. A total of 4,183 houses and flats were provided between the two world wars, and this vigorous policy was adopted again as soon as possible after the end of hostilities in 1945. Parks, and recreation and sports facilities were provided; public transport was brought up to date, with tramways, trolleybuses, and (nearly eighty) motor-buses introduced in sequence; attention was given to matters concerning public health, including the purchase in 1893 of a large extension to the 1855 burial-ground on the outskirts of the town, and the establishment of a crematorium in 1927.

The Rural Districts, though their resources were inevitably smaller, made correspondingly good progress. Several 'cottage' hospitals were founded (at Felixstowe, in 1909, for example). Amenities such as playing-fields, mobile library services, street lighting, and better schemes of sewage-disposal, helped the villages, and a number obtained grants towards providing or improving their village halls. Woodbridge, Hadleigh, Sudbury, and Halesworth have all built swimming-pools in recent years. West Suffolk in particular carried out an extensive and successful programme of organizing holiday play schemes, with a wide range of activities, providing the necessary premises and equipment. This was

Bury St Edmunds: Robert Adam's Town Hall is now the Market Cross Exhibition Gallery

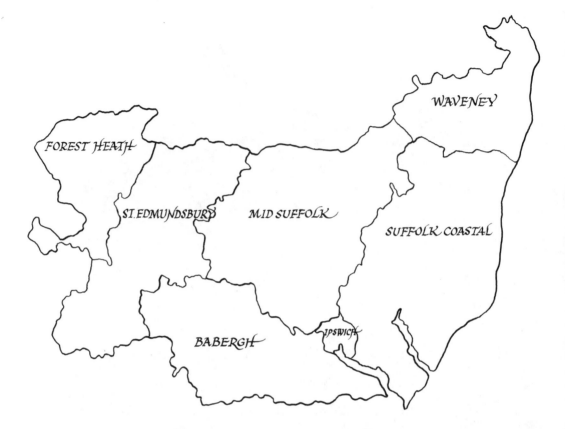

one good example of an active and productive partnership between voluntary organizations and local authorities.

A new Suffolk County Council was elected on 12 April 1973: it took over the functions of the former East and West Suffolk County Councils and some of those of the Ipswich County Borough Council. This new Council is responsible for a wide range of services, including education, planning, the fire and police services, and the social services. The responsibilities of the District Councils are more specifically local, and they have acquired from the former county authorities the vitally important powers of 'planning control', the decisions about the location and the quality of all new building in the Districts. They are also responsible for such matters as the protection of the coast, and environmental health services (the old Public Health Department). Two more authorities, created in the 1974 reorganization, are the Anglian Water Authority and the Suffolk Area Health Authority. Their functions are shown in the Table opposite.

Both the county and district councillors are elected by the public for terms of four years. The old system of electing parish councillors remains unchanged. There are regular meetings of all authorities, both of the whole Council, for important policy decisions, and of sub-committees of councillors who are responsible for the particular services operated by the Council. Like this, councillors may be able to specialize in the work of a committee in which they are especially interested. Their recommendations on matters of policy can be put forward to the full Council for its consideration and attention.

The money to provide all the local government services (and the considerable cost of administering them) is raised partly through the rating system, partly through grants from the Government at Westminster, and – a very small proportion – from some of the services provided, such as rents from council houses, or the admission charges at swimming-pools.

The Suffolk County Council

Main functions	Departmental head
Education, careers advice, sport and recreation	County Education Officer
Social services (children, old people, the disabled, etc.)	Director of Social Services
Highways, waste disposal, transport co-ordination, road safety, street lighting, footpaths	County Surveyor
Libraries	County Librarian
Archives and records	County Archivist
Consumer protection (weights and measures, trades descriptions, explosives and petroleum storage)	County Consumer Protection Officer
County farms, valuation, estate management	County Land Agent and Valuer
Strategic and land-use planning	County Planning Officer
Financial affairs (insurances, investments, superannuation)	County Treasurer
Administration, personnel, legal services, rent officers, registrars, coroners, animal and plant diseases	County Secretary
Fire	County Fire Officer
Police	Chief Constable
Policy, management and co-ordination	Chief Executive

The District Councils

Housing, building regulations, some street-lighting and highways responsibility

Local planning control, and land use

Environmental health – slaughterhouses, food safety and hygiene, home safety, noise control, clean air, some sewerage responsibility

Sport, recreation, and leisure services – parks, open spaces, swimming-pools, museums, concert-halls, holiday amenities

Coast protection

Airports

Elections and electoral registration

Parish Councils

Burial-grounds

Allotments

Some highway functions, e.g. maintenance and signposting of footpaths, footway lighting, off-street car parking

Suffolk Area Health Authority

Hospitals, clinics, midwives, nursing, ambulances

Anglian Water Authority

Water-supply, sewerage, sewage disposal, land drainage